WebMaster

How To Build Your Own World Wide Web Server
Without Really Trying

WebMaster

Windows®

How To Build Your Own
World Wide Web Server
Without Really Trying

Bob LeVitus
Jeff Evans

AP PROFESSIONAL

Boston San Diego New York
London Sydney Tokyo Toronto

AP PROFESSIONAL
1300 Boylston Street, Chestnut Hill, MA 02167

An imprint of ACADEMIC PRESS, INC.
A Division of HARCOURT BRACE & COMPANY

United Kingdom Edition published by
ACADEMIC PRESS LIMITED
24–28 Oval Road, London NW1 7DX

ISBN 0-12-445572-7

Printed in the United States of America
95 96 97 98   IP   9 8 7 6 5 4 3 2 1

For Allison and Jacob, my wonderful little WebSurfers-in-training

— Bob LeVitus

For my parents and sisters—for Kathy, Mikey, and our one on the way

— Jeff Evans

CONTENTS

Introduction

IN THE BEGINNING

The Authors Speak ...

By now you've probably read or seen dozens if not hundreds of books about the Internet — what it's all about, how to get started, and where to go once you get there. You've spent the past few months moving up the admittedly steep learning curve of the Net, getting your SLIP or PPP account configured just so, reading books and magazine articles, and firing up your cool tools like Internet in Box, Chameleon, or Netscape. (Well, OK, maybe you prefer Mosaic and are still fiddling around with different signature lines in Eudora ... Still, you know what we mean.)

WebMaster Windows is something completely different, something new, something exciting — a book about building your own WWW (World Wide Web) server without really trying. So welcome to our book. In just a few hundred easy-to-understand pages we promise to teach you everything you need to know (and we mean *everything*) to turn your PC into a World Wide Web site on the Internet. Without really trying. Really.

(While we're at it, and for no extra charge, we'll show you how to set up a bunch of other cool stuff once your PC is up as a server on the Net. We'll also provide the URLs of dozens of interesting Web sites you can check out for inspiration. So don't touch that dial.)

Acknowledgments

Before we go any further, there are several acknowledgments we have to make. Most of all we want to thank Robert Denny for developing NCSA HTTPd for Windows. Without HTTPd for Windows, WebMastery would be excruciatingly painful for the average person — and expensive. HTTPd for Windows is a great piece of enabling technology — like the spreadsheet or the word processor — that opens up entire new computing vistas. It lets you do things you never thought you'd do—namely, design and run a Web site with a minimum of fuss and bother, and NO UNIX WHATSOEVER!

You should know right off the bat that there are a couple of ways to go about setting your PC up as a Web site. We suggest you take the easy approach to begin with and use Quarterdeck's WebServer™. You have a few options when it comes to choosing the software to run your Web site, but WebServer is the one we are going to cover. It is a simple and affordable approach and doesn't require much in the way of hardware or software other than a PC running Windows. It is also on the CD-ROM you received with this book. From there, depending on what you need to accomplish, you can look into running a Windows NT-based Web server and use O'Reilly's WebSite™, Netscape Communication's NetSite™ or one of the other commercial Web server packages for the PC. With a few more late nights and some big-time noodling you can even turn your PC into a UNIX box and be a full-service Internet provider — a subject beyond the scope of this book.

We don't recommend that you run off and dive into the cost of setting up a Windows NT Web server or try to tackle the complexity of running UNIX on your PC if you're just getting started. Far from it. In fact, we think it's better to move up the curve gradually using the equipment you already own and freely available software. There is a lot to digest and this book is meant to be fun for the average PC user.

In a nutshell, WebServer will let you get your Web site up and running without really trying. So, of course, we've included the latest version — at press time — of Webserver on the CD that accompanies this book. You can always pick up the latest version of this most essential tool at WebMaster Windows WWW server at **http://www. webmasterwin.com.**

Finally, thanks to all the master-blaster WebMasters who helped make this book possible, in particular, Jon Weiderspan at the University of Washington and Stephen Collins at the University of Minnesota College of Education. These two were instrumental in helping us learn the stuff we're about to teach. Be sure to check out their WWW and FTP sites listed in our hot lists, which are also included on the CD that came with this book.

Who This Book Is For

WebMaster Windows is for anyone who is reasonably proficient with their PC and wants their own Web page. You don't have to be a programmer or a "DOS-Head." Neither of us is. Jeff can barely figure out the autoexec.bat file, let alone Visual Basic, and Bob isn't all that much better though he's been writing about Windows for almost as long as he's been writing about the Mac. You don't have to be a big-time network administrator or UNIX geek either. We're not. All you need is a little imagination, an Internet account, and this book and CD.

If you know how to turn on your PC and launch files, just kick back, follow along, and you'll be mastering your own Web site RealSoonNow (as they say in the software business). Trust us — we're trained professionals.

How to Use This Book

If you already have a SLIP, PPP, or dedicated Internet account and are ready to jump right in, skip forward a few chapters and go for it. It wouldn't hurt you to at least skim the earlier chapters, though. There's a lot in them; you may not know it all.

We wrote this book so you'd have a great tutorial and great reference book. (It's two, two, two books in one.) The tutorials are totally original, made up by the two of us, but a lot of the reference material can also be found on the Net — somewhere. If you know where to look. We've tried to recap the best of it here to save you the trouble.

But ... (and Isn't There Always a "But"?)

But there are a few excellent sites WinWebMasters should visit regularly; we'll tell you about them later in this tome and why you should visit them often. When *we* started to set up our PCs as Web servers, it was a pain in the you-know-what to surf all over the place on the Internet trying to find everything we needed and wanted to know. We found it easy to get lost or distracted, and, depending on your service plan and degree of addiction, it can get expensive surfing the ether at 14.4 baud. So, throughout this book, we'll try our best to save you the trouble and only steer you toward the best, brightest, and most worthwhile sites.

Overview (with a Point of View)

Let's take a look at where we're headed.

We'll start with a quick (we promise) overview of the Internet in general and the Web in particular. What makes our viewpoint unique, we think, is that it focuses on the origin and growth of the World Wide Web, rather than telling the hackneyed old "you've heard it a million times" tale of the history of the Internet (i.e., ARPA, Department of Defense, university researchers, huge growth rates, cover of *Newsweek*, blah, blah, blah). Try it — you might even enjoy it.

In Defense of Words on Paper...

It's embarrassing how many times we printed out documentation for one of these Internet tools, so we could read through it at our leisure, off-line and sans computer. Hypertext on screen is well and good, but you can lose your place easily when scrolling and clicking through screen after screen. In other words, there's something to be said for a good old-fashioned book like this one. (OK, old-fashioned books didn't come with CD-ROMs, but you know what we mean.)

A book is a wonderful thing. It feels good to hold. It doesn't require electricity or batteries. You can slap a Post-It™ note on a key page or passage. You can grab it off the shelf and refer to it easily, without waiting for your computer to boot up. You can throw it at your dog. And it's easier to use in the bathroom than a laptop or notebook computer.

On the other hand, portions of this book can be found on the WebMaster Windows server (**http://www.webmasterwin.com**, if you've forgotten) formatted as Web pages, complete with links. Let's see a paperback do that!

Bottom line: Hypertext is nifty, but books are cool, too. There's plenty of room for both in the world.

From the history and growth of the WWW we move on to more concrete issues such as server connectivity with your Internet provider and an overview of the Web client-server architecture. It's more nutsy-and-boltsy than the aforementioned history lesson, but it's not as boring as it sounds.

After that we delve deeper into Web page design. We've lined up some great contributions from experts on both aesthetic and information design, so even if you consider yourself artistically challenged, like Bob, you'll pick up valuable pointers here.

That's followed by an intense lesson in writing great HTML code with tips and hints from master WebMasters. We'll show you some great examples of how it's done, and some great examples of how *not* to do it.

Then there's the step-by-step walkthrough: how to set up your Web server using Quarterdeck's WebServer one step at a time. Don't worry; it's easier than you could possibly believe. If you can read it, you can do it. You'll be up and running in no time.

In the closing stretch we'll do a quick bit of geeky stuff and check out the Windows NT Web server scene. Finally, we wrap it all up with a glimpse of the future, and what some famous Netheads think the Web might be like a few years from now.

Pay the Piper on That Shareware

OK. Let's be honest with each other. Many of us have used shareware that we didn't pay for. We're all guilty of it at one time or another. Let's turn over a new leaf. In other words, we're asking you to please pay the developer if you regularly use any of the shareware that comes with this book.

We don't know of any developers making a living off shareware fees, so give 'em a break. They worked hard on that software. If you use the shareware, pay the registration fee. Please.

We know it's a hassle to write a check and mail it. (Just think, soon you'll be able to do it all via the Web.) But for now, you'll have to do it the old-fashioned way — one envelope at a time. But please do at least consider doing it. It'll make you, as well as the developer, feel better.

Our Promise

Here's our promise to you, faithful reader. This book will be the easiest, most understandable, most logical, and most convenient way to get a Windows Web site up and running. It's that simple.

Keeping in Touch with Us

You can stay current by accessing the WebMaster Windows WWW server at **http://www.webmasterwin.com**. Relax, breathe — we'll be there with the latest, greatest versions of Win WebMaster development tools and tips. We'll also have all the latest Win Net apps, all the relevant newsgroups, listservs, URLs, our monthly hot lists—you name it. If it has to do with running a better Web site, it will be there. All in one place! So stop by often.

So there you have it. Have fun, and don't forget to send us the address of your WWW site when it's up and running!

Last but not least, please let us know how you liked this book.

Peace.

Bob LeVitus
levitus@onr.com

and

Jeff Evans
jevans@outer.net

Chapter 1

THE HISTORY OF THE WORLD WIDE WEB (WWW)

What It Is, How Big It Is, and Why You Need to Know This Stuff

Though it's sometimes said that size doesn't matter, when it comes to the Internet and World Wide Web, there are some compelling reasons for knowing approximately how many denizens are out there. It's important for you to have some sort of handle on just how big the Internet is and what part of the overall traffic is Web traffic in order to help you plan your own Web site. After all, just as you wouldn't want to throw a party and not know how many people might show up, you don't want to open shop on the Web without some idea of how much activity to expect.

So we'll tackle that issue in this chapter, and while we're at it, we'll take a look at the brief history of the Web as we know it.

But First, a Quick Brag about Our Home Town

We are fortunate to live in Austin, Texas. Besides being a fabulous place to live, Austin is a hotbed of Internet activity, Internet providers, and World Wide Web sites.

For what it's worth, Austin has at least half a dozen PC manufacturers, and is the home of:

- Microelectronics and Computer Technology Corporation (MCC), where WinWeb was developed, and home of EINet Galaxy Web Server.
- HAL Computer Services, where David Connolly is instrumental in putting together specifications for future versions of HTML (and where you can test your own HTML; more on that later).
- A dozen or more Internet providers.
- A couple of Internet Special Interest groups including the Austin Web Users Group (AWUG).
- The University of Texas (Hook 'em Horns!), itself a hotbed of Internet activity in general and WWW in particular.

and...

- The Iron Works and the Salt Lick, perhaps the finest BBQ restaurants on the planet.

The Complete (Ha, ha) History of Growth

In researching the history of the Web and its growth rate in relation to the Internet itself, we turned to local experts John Quarterman and Smoot Carl-Mitchell of Texas Internet Consulting (TIC). John and Smoot may be Austinites, but they are recognized worldwide as authorities on quantifying the size and growth of the Internet.

Their work is prolific — each year they put together the *TIC/MIDS Internet Demographic Study,* the result of months and months of "pinging" sites and digging through Internet IP traffic reports. Their approach is both scientific and technical.

How Big Is It? (The Internet)

There has been more than a little discussion of just how big the Internet actually is. (For that matter, there's been more than a little discussion of *what* the Internet actually is, but that's a topic best tackled in someone else's book.) For our purposes, suffice it to say that the Users Services Working Group of the Internet Engineering Task Force (IETF) made one of the first "official" stabs at defining the Internet in one of its Requests for Comments (RFCs), way back in May 1993. Here's what they said:

> The Internet can be thought about in relation to its common protocols, as a physical collection of routers and circuits, as a set of shared resources, or even as an attitude about interconnecting and intercommunications. Some common definitions in the past include:
>
> - a network of networks based on the TCP/IP protocols
> - a community of people who use and develop those networks
> - a collection of resources that can be reached from those networks
>
> Today's Internet is a global resource connecting millions of users that began as an experiment over 20 years ago by the US Department of Defense. While the networks that make up the Internet are based on a standard set of protocols (a mutually agreed upon method of communication between parties), the Internet also has gateways to networks and services that are based on other protocols.
>
> —RFC 1462

By the way, if you want more than that by way of definition, we recommend Ed Krol's excellent book, *The Whole Internet User's Guide and Catalog* (O'Reilly & Associates; $29.95.)

But What's It Done Lately?

What's been happening since RFC 1462 was written two years ago? Gateways to networks and services based on other protocols have been changing dramatically. Private, corporate, and commercial online networks are gaining more and better access to the full range of Internet protocols and services.

These days you have to include commercial services like CompuServe, America Online (AOL), Genie, and Delphi — and all their users — as part of the Internet. You also have to count the other networks, subnetworks, and BBSs included in John and Smoot's so-called "matrix" of networks — things like FidoNet and BitNet, and BBS systems like First-Class and ResNova with Internet eMail, UseNet, Telnet, FTP, and WWW server capability. Then you have to include the private enterprise networks of large corporations such as Exxon and Motorola that use the Internet Protocol (IP) for their internal network services and data communications. And finally, don't forget to count all the university and college students on campus-wide networks that are plugged into the Internet.

The Internet Index

The Internet Index is a lighthearted look at things Internet, inspired by "Harper's Index" and compiled by Win Treese (treese@OpenMarket.com).

Here's Internet Index #5, reproduced by permission:

Growth of Gopher traffic in 1993	1076%
Growth of Gopher traffic in 1994	197%
Growth of WWW traffic in 1993	443,931%
Growth of WWW traffic in 1994	1713%
Growth in NSFnet traffic in 1994	110%
Advertised network numbers in November 1993	19,664

The Internet Index (continued)

Advertised network numbers in November 1994   42,883
Source: Merit Statistics

Number of Internet access providers with service in Quito, Ecuador   1
Source: Network USA Internet Service Providers Catalog

Number of countries reachable by electronic mail in 1993   137*

Number of countries reachable by electronic mail in 1994   159*
Source: Larry Landweber's International Connectivity Table

Number of countries on the Internet in 1993   60

Number of countries on the Internet in 1994   60
Source: Larry Landweber's International Connectivity Table

Number of sites participating in "First Night in Cyberspace"   10
Source: Cyberfoo

Number of peer-reviewed scholarly journals published electronically on the Internet   over 70
Source: Peter Fox and Jack Lancaster, "Neuroscience on the Net," Science, 11/11/94, pp 994–996

Number of attendees at Internet World, Jan. 1992   272

Number of attendees at Internet World, Dec. 1994   over 10,000
Source: Alan Meckler

Number of "cybercafes" in the United Kingdom   1
Source: Cyberia

Number of subscribers to the ClariNet electronic newspaper   80,000
Source: ClariNet

Number of FBI cases officially publicized on the Internet   1
Source: Federal Bureau of Investigation

Percentage increase in weight of the 2nd edition of the Canadian Internet Handbook   280
Source: Jim Carroll

*approximate

The Internet Index (continued)	
Number of meetings of the Internet Engineering Task Force, through 1994 *Source: IETF*	31
Number of US Youth Soccer teams with web pages *Source: US Soccer WWW Page (suggested by John Kinney)*	2
On average, number of days between issuing of new Internet RFCs in 1994	2
Number of phone calls to InterNIC Registration Services during Nov. 1994 *Source: November Internet Monthly Report*	1,964
Number of Internet messages causing Microsoft to issue a press release denying them	1

"Harper's Index" is a registered trademark of Harper's Magazine Foundation. Internet Index © 1994 by Win Treese. Send updates or interesting statistics to treese@OpenMarket.com. To subscribe to future issues of the Internet Index, send a message saying "subscribe internet-index" in the body to: **internet-index-request@OpenMarket.com.**

And so, depending on how you define the Internet, it is generally agreed these days that the number of Internet users is somewhere between 20 and 30 million. (Though there are several advertising and PR firms that haven't figured it out yet, and are still quoting the front page *New York Times* article from the Fall of '94, which put the number of Internet users — erroneously — at about 2 million.)

No, YOU Do It!

If you don't believe us and the higher number we tout, check out D. C. Dennison and the staff of the Global Network Navigator's *GNN U-DO-It Internet Estimator.* You'll see that it agrees with us.

Between the time we finish writing this book and it gets from the publisher to you, the definition of what it means to be a user on the Internet will become even more blurred and the number of users will be

U-Do-It Internet Estimator

The *GNN U-Do-It Estimator* is a quick and dirty way to sketch out the size of the Internet. Follow GNN's advice and use a pencil. They take the total number of hosts on the Internet — about 3.8 million according to Mark Lottor's monthly Internet Domain Survey. Then they get conservative and subtract all the host computers behind corporate "firewall" security schemes — minus 2.5 million. Then they add back that 2.5 million since they agree with Quarterman that corporate users consume Internet bandwidth resources and can still do eMail, net news, and the like even though you and I can't get in. So we're still at 3.8 million, right? (What an exercise they make of all this.). Next the *U-Do-It Estimator* takes Quarterman's estimate of the number of users per host machine on the Net such as friends, students, and dogs on the Net when the owner is not around (3.8). Then you add 4 to 5 million or so for people who are on all the online and eMail services such as AOL, CompuServe, and MCIMail and 4 to 5 million for all the other types of network users that can and do use Internet resources (FidoNet, BITNET, UUCP, and the like). When your head is done spinning you end up with a number around 20 to 25 million. They should call it the *U-Go-Ahead-and-Do-It-For-Me Internet Estimator.*

Of course, if your computer has an early-model Pentium chip, you may get a different number entirely.

Sorry. We couldn't resist.

even higher. And just wait until the cable television companies figure it out and are approved to bring high-speed Internet access right to your TV…. You see what we mean. Suffice it to say that the Internet is huge and growing bigger by the minute.

How Big Is It? (The World Wide Web)

It's big. If the Internet is growing fast, the World Wide Web is growing as fast or faster. The generally accepted growth rate for the Internet is about 100% per year. At that rate, according to John Quarterman, everyone will be connected to the Internet by the year 2003.

Get Real, John ...

OK, hang on. Let's get real. It's not going to continue at that rate and we won't all be connected in eight years. But, as we've already demonstrated, the Internet is big and growing fast. And the point we're about to make is that the World Wide Web is big and is growing as fast as or faster than the Internet as a whole.

We'll get back to exactly how big after a brief discussion of what the Web actually is ...

Brief Discourse: What Exactly Is This Web Thing, Anyway?

So what's the big deal about this here World Wide Web? What has made it so popular? We'd say it's that the Web provides a point and click, graphical interface that can take you from place to place in cyberspace. (Unless, of course, you're browsing the Web with Lynx, like an old-time UNIX geek).

The Web is easy and the Web is fun. It's also the most coherent and easily accessible way to get information on the Internet. And these days, just about everything on the Net can be viewed through the glasses of a Web site. Modern Web browsers can do Gopher, WAIS, FTP, UseNet, Telnet, electronic mail, and more. We've even seen a variation of Chat on the Web.

The Web was started by some scientists at CERN, who set out to build a big distributed hypermedia system and have succeeded in a manner beyond their wildest dreams.

CERN Who? You Must Be That Boson from Mars.

The more-or-less official birth of the Web was in 1989 at CERN, the European Center for Particle Physics, located near Geneva, Switzerland. From the get-go, the needs of particle physicists have made CERN a leader in networking technologies. All those physicists from around the world collaborating on complex physics, engineering, and information handling projects needed a way to share info efficiently. The Web was the result.

Most recently CERN and MIT have gotten together to help provide guidelines for the continued development of standards for the Web. Out of that has come the W3 Consortium. The W3C is an international industry-sponsored effort that has basically the same goals as CERN and MIT. Some of the early companies to join include: AT&T, Digital Equipment Corporation, Enterprise Integration Technologies, FTP Software, Hummingbird Communication, IBM, IXI, MCI, Mosaic Communications, NCSA, Open Market, O'Reilly Associates, Spyglass, and Sun Microsystems.

You can find out more about the W3 Consortium at **http://www10.w3.org/hypertext/WWW/Consortium/Prospectus/**

Hypertext Is the Key

What makes the Web so incredibly cool is hypertext and its stepsister, hypermedia (pictures, sound, movies, etc.). This hyper stuff is what makes the Web what it is.

When you're surfing the Web and you need more information on a subject you're reading about, you just click on a word or image that is a hyperlink and you're automatically transported to another page or site on the Internet that has additional information. It's kind of like foot-notes with hard-wired cross-references to the actual referenced document — words, pictures, movies, or sounds. The really cool part is that the linked document can reside on the other side of the world on a different computer.

The "hyper-ness" of the Web makes the whole more than the sum of the parts. Imagine a James Michener novel on a Web site with hyper-text links to all the historical references and places mentioned in each chapter. The possibilities are endless — especially as the nature of hyper-media itself gets extended.

Hold that thought for later; we'll be talking a lot about designing good hypertext and hypermedia documents in just a few chapters. For now, the bottom line is that with the use of hypertext and hypermedia the Internet instantly became a really fun place to hang out.

With the advent of the Web, the Internet became more than eMail and file transfers and command-line interfaces. It became more than UNIX. Suddenly, using the Internet *was like using Windows*. You just point and click and it works. Cool.

OK, So How Big Is the Web???

The reason we dwelt on the size of the Internet is to blow your mind about what's happening with the size and growth of the Web. In relation to the amount of Net activity comprised of eMail, FTP, UseNet, and so on, the Web size and growth curve is awesome. In November 1994 alone, the number of WWW packets traveling over the Internet increased by 48%, or 10% per week! No other type of traffic — eMail, FTP, Gopher, WAIS, etc. — on the Internet came close to the traffic of the Web.

Growing like a WWWeed

We asked Stephen Collins at the University of Minnesota to give us an idea of how much increase in Web traffic there was on the Net last year. Here's what he told us:

The data I have charted is from samples taken from the NSF backbone. The NSFnet represents a portion of the main Internet backbone. Any calculation of "total" Internet traffic would be guestimates at best. However, the percentages of NSFnet traffic are probably a pretty good indication of the percentage on the Internet as a whole.

You can measure traffic in terms of "bytes" or "packets" and get very different figures.

For example, with the Telnet protocol, there are a large number of packets with only one character.

With the FTP protocol, packets are almost always full (~1500 bytes).

The dismantling of NSFnet began in the final months of 1994, so the NSF total statistics actually showed a decline. Most certainly, the numbers below do not reflect the Internet as a whole, which has seen nothing but sharp increases in traffic.

All told, I think my figures and graphs from the NSF statistics for 1994 are a fairly accurate picture of the Internet.

Here are some of the WWW totals from the NSF statistics:

Month	Bytes		Packets	
	Total	%	Total	%
1 Jan 93	511,450	0.00	122,440,450	0.00
1 Jan 94	822,317,950	1.49	269,129,084,100	2.61
1 Jan 95	11,518,306,800	13.12	3,382,697,720,400	17.69

I'd measure by bytes myself, which gives you an 880% increase in the percentage, and about a 1400% increase in total WWW traffic.

—*Stephen E. Collins*
University of Minnesota
sec@boombox.micro.umn.edu

Looked at another way, at the end of 1994 there were more than 10,000 Web servers on the Internet according to Matthew Gray's World Wide Web Wanderer; two years before that there were probably fewer than 500. (There'll be at least 10,001 once yours is up and running.)

Since Web browsing software such as Mosaic, Netscape, and WinWeb were introduced and distributed freely, millions and millions of these and other popular "browsers" have been downloaded or distributed. That means millions and millions of users surfing the Web. Doug Colbeth, the president of the commercial software company Spyglass (the master licensee of Mosaic) said last year that they alone had licensed 10 million copies of Mosaic to more than 20 commercial concerns.

It's much easier to get a handle on the size of Web traffic on the Net in relation to the total amount of Net traffic by means of a graph. Measuring Net traffic by protocol type — FTP (file transfers), SMTP (mail), NNTP (news) — is easy if you have the time. Just go to **gopher:// nic.merit.edu** and get buried in the latest numbers and make some graphs like Stephen Collins did (see Figures 1.1 to 1.5).

Figure 1.1: *Average daily IP packet count.*
Source: Stephen Collins, University of Minnesota, December 1994.

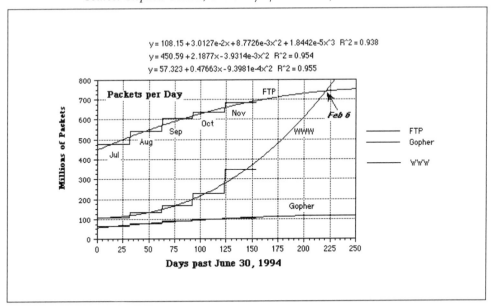

Figure 1.2: *Total IP traffic by type in bytes.*
Source: Stephen Collins, University of Minnesota, December 1994.

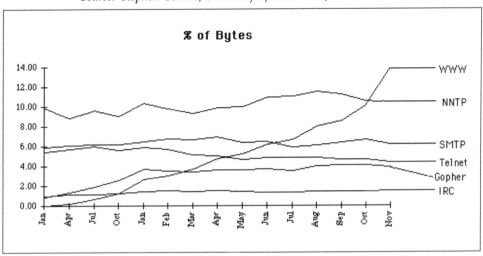

Figure 1.3: *WWW vs. Gopher in bytes.*

Source: Stephen Collins, University of Minnesota, December 1994.

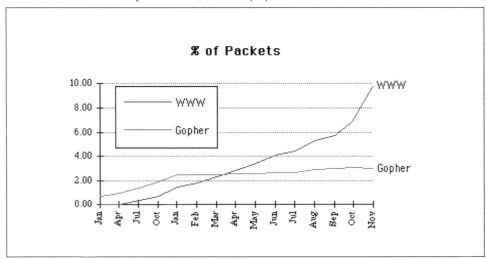

Figure 1.4: *WWW vs. Gopher in packets.*

Source: Stephen Collins, University of Minnesota, December 1994.

Figure 1.5: *Total bytes transferred in absolute numbers.*
Source: Stephen Collins, University of Minnesota, December 1994.

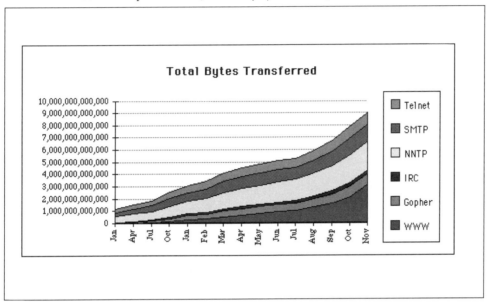

Summary and Conclusion

That wasn't so bad, was it? Well, that's it. You're done with the history lesson. You got the idea, right? It's big. And a lot of people are surfing it.

If you need more on the size and growth of the Internet and WWW then take a cruise to the World Wide Web Wanderer Web site at **http:// www.mit.edu:8001/people/mkgray/web-growth.html**. You can also check out the CyberWeb Virtual Library sponsored by the Maryland-based Internet provider, CharmNet. The URL is **http://www.charm.net/ ~web/Vlib/Misc/Statistics.html**. If you're really twisted and just can't live without the raw data, you can find it at **gopher://nic.merit.edu: 7043/1/nsfnet/statistics.**

The whole history of the Net and WWW is fascinating. People do nothing but study and collect data on it every day. Not us — and probably not you. It's there if you want it and you can use it to help justify or build a marketing story for what is the most exciting thing happening on the Net — setting up and running a WWW server.

In the next chapter you're going to get your feet wet. We're going to review the basic system requirements you need to have in place and take a look at the connectivity side of things. You'll learn what to ask for from your Internet provider and you'll pick up some tips on managing the relationship. You're also going to learn what the whole client–server story is all about.

Sound like a plan? OK, then kick back, relax, and turn the page …

Chapter 2

GETTING YOUR FEET WET

Connections, Providers, Speed, TCP/IP,
a (Brief) Client–Server Story, and a Hands-On Tutorial

This chapter is about Internet providers, setting up your connection with an Internet provider, and your speed options for connecting. Along the way we'll tell you a little about network protocols and the client–server story and a bit about the UNIX operating system and what makes UNIX lovers tick.

Then (and only then) we'll start our hands-on festivities with a delightful little ditty we call the WebServer Quick Start.

To Surf and Provide: The Service Provider Story

If you're going to be a WebMaster, the most important person in your life is your Internet service provider. This section will tell you a little about the species, but in a nutshell, here's our advice: Cherish them and treat them right.

On Dealing with UNIX and UNIX Geeks

UNIX is the indecipherable multi-user, multi-tasking, multi-platform operating system that's more or less the standard for the Internet. Most service providers use high-powered computer workstations running the UNIX operating system.

Traditionally, Windows and UNIX have had an uneasy relationship. "UNIX is impossible for mere mortals to use" vs. "Windows isn't really an operating system." But given the fact that many of the machines on the Net are running UNIX, it's obvious that we Windows enthusiasts must learn to get along with the UNIX community.

Just between us, the Windows interface is better than UNIX's cryptic commands. And PCs are a zillion times easier to use. The truth is, there's less and less that you can do with a UNIX box that you can't do just as well or better on a PC. But you'll never convince a dyed-in-the-wool UNIX geek of that. And chances are good that your service provider is dyed-in-the-wool.

So if your service provider is comfortable with the UNIX command line, don't try to convince him or her to run the site on a PC with Windows. Trust us, you can't.

Follow this simple rule and you'll have a long, mutually beneficial relationship with your provider; disobey it and you'll have a screaming match that neither of you has the slightest possibility of winning.

The Early Days When Life Was Simple (Not!)

Let's say it right up front: TCP/IP and UNIX are ugly. They're decidedly user-unfriendly. In the early days, we mostly got our Internet accounts from UNIX geeks who didn't get it. They figured that we "little computer" users would know how to configure TCP/IP. Wrong! They thought we would be able to write our own modem scripts for our SLIP or PPP software. Wrong again. It wasn't long before they were swamped with support calls from PC users.

Things are better these days. Most Internet providers give you a nice, customized installer disk with everything preconfigured for your SLIP or PPP dial-up connection. Just double-click and the installer sets all the IP addressing information in your TCP/IP stack automatically, and prompts you to choose your modem brand and type from a pop-up menu and to enter your user ID and password. Then, just click the Connect button and away you surf!

OK, not every Internet provider is that savvy. But things today are much better. Our advice: If your provider can't at least preconfigure your SLIP or PPP software for you, think about changing providers.

Your Internet Provider Is Your Friend

Have you ever been over to your Internet provider's offices and seen their hardware? Have you ever met them in person? If not, you should. Have them show you their setup and explain which box does what. Get to know the people who work there. Take a UNIX geek to lunch. Trust us, it'll be worth it someday when you've got major problems on your end.

All kidding aside, it's extremely important to be on good terms with your Internet provider or your network administrator. There is much they can do to make setting up and running your Web site go even easier; you'll be depending on them for configuring your setup, getting a permanent address on the Internet, and maintaining the physical connection between your site and theirs. So do be nice.

Believe us, as soon as your network or ISDN connection goes down, you're going to be calling the expert for help. The whole thing is so much easier if that expert is also your friend. We can't begin to emphasize this enough.

A Typical Internet Site

Here's the setup for one of the Internet providers we know in Austin. The machine names and IP numbers have been changed to protect the innocent.

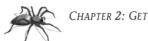

It's not that complicated, really. Just gaze at Figure 2.1 and, in your mind, add about a ton of wires running all over the place and some guys who seem a little out-there and bug-eyed wild wearing jeans and T-shirts who haven't slept or combed their hair in days because they are setting up so many new accounts. Nice picture, eh?

Getting What You Need from Your Internet Provider to Get Started

There are two things you need to get from your Internet provider or network administrator to get your Web page up and running. The first is a

Figure 2.1: *Internet site layout, Tomorrow's Technologies, Austin, Texas, January 1995.*

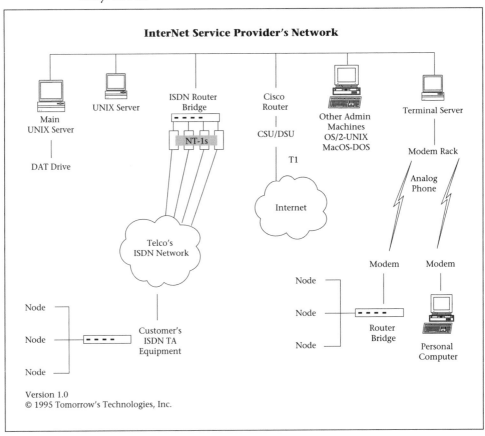

dedicated, permanent connection to the Internet; the second is a permanent address on the Internet itself. If you haven't got both, these are two items you must have if you want to run a real full-time Web site. Realistically it takes two to three weeks to get this stuff in place, so read what follows, then contact your Internet provider and get started ASAP.

If you are already connected to the Net full-time and have a permanent Internet address, skim the next couple of pages (but don't miss the jokes and secret passwords).

Inexpensive Connection Choices

Like we said, if you are serious about setting up a Web site you are going to need to get some sort of dedicated 24-hour connection from your Internet provider. Unless you're doing an in-house Web site for your company and only need the site to be available during specific hours, it's kind of bogus to set up a Web site, announce it to the world, and then not have it available 24 hours a day.

There are a couple of ways to go and several things to keep in mind when you're deciding what type of connection to get. Basically your connection choices are:

- An analog line using a 14.4K or 28.8K bps modem, or
- A digital line such as a 56K dedicated line, Frame Relay, ISDN, or a T1 (faster than that and you're really talking big money).

The cost for a dedicated connection will range from $75 a month to more than $5000 per month, depending on which type of line you choose. Prices keep dropping, so ask your Internet provider for the latest rates.

We've included a list of Internet providers by major metropolitan area as an appendix. Better still, you can usually get a current list off the Net itself by posting to a UseNet newsgroup for the city you live in; in our case we'd ask in Austin.general. Post a message something like this:

"I'm looking for a local Internet provider who offers ISDN [or whatever type of connection you want] at reasonable rates. I'd appreciate any recommendations. Thanks."

The type of connectivity you go with depends on your need for speed, your budget, and how many "hits" a day you anticipate your site is going to get. We'll talk about your options in depth in a moment. Keep in mind that many people hitting your site will be using a 14.4K or 28.8K modem connection at their end. If there are a lot of people hitting your site simultaneously or if you are serving up large images, you're going to want a faster connection to handle the traffic and maintain performance. Choose a slow connection and people will come to your site, wait around too long for some text or image to load, say "later," and surf away. It's easy just to click away from a slow site — easier than flipping channels, watching six shows at once, and driving your wife crazy. Tuck this little tidbit away in the back of your mind for now; we'll talk more about it later.

Anyway, the need for speed is something that's hard to predict. We recommend you start out modestly. You can always add bandwidth later. On the other hand, let's get real and stop beating around the bush: Get as much bandwidth as you can possibly afford. Like RAM and hard-disk space, more is always better.

Dedicated Modem

We recommend starting out with a dedicated 28.8K modem connection. Check with your Internet provider to see if they offer it; almost all do these days. You'll need a V.42bis modem, a phone line, and a dedicated SLIP or PPP account with your service provider.

This type of connection is typically the least expensive. Bearing in mind that prices are always changing (usually dropping), V.42bis modems are going for around $200 as we write this in mid-1995. Most Internet providers are offering dedicated 28.8 connections for under $100 a month. By the way, 28.8 is probably as fast as it's going to get over analog phone lines. For higher performance, you'll need to move to digital lines such as ISDN or T1 (explained in the next section).

To sum up the costs: a V.32bis modem, a standard analog phone line that you don't use for anything else, plus setup and monthly fees you'll pay to your Internet provider. All in all, a dedicated 28.8K connection should cost you a couple of hundred dollars to get up and running, and a couple of hundred a month to maintain.

The Great Debate: SLIP vs. PPP

We recommend that if you are going the dedicated 28.8K modem route, that you stay away from SLIP (Serial Line Interface Protocol) and look for a provider who offers PPP (Point to Point Protocol). You don't need to know much about them but here's what you *do* need to know:

PPP allows multiple protocols concurrently over a dial-up link. You want that. We prefer PPP over SLIP because PPP gives you more flexibility, is more robust, and has more new development being done for it than SLIP. In fact, we'd venture to say that SLIP is becoming less prevalent and is usually more of a nuisance to configure.

So our advice — if you don't already have a satisfactory connection — is find a provider who offers dedicated PPP connections for V.32bis modems.

The Importance of a Permanent Address

SLIP and PPP implementations pretty much provide equivalent access to the Internet by allowing your PC to be used with a modem to turn it into a machine that is "on the Net."

When you connect to go surfing the Net with a SLIP or PPP connection, you receive an "IP address" assigned by the UNIX box at your Internet provider. That address is in effect for the duration of your dial-up session. (Really. You can check it out any time by opening Winsock or whatever stack you are using during your session to see what IP address has been assigned.) Each time you dialed in you may have received a different IP address.

Since in the past you were *surfing* the Net and not serving a Web page on the Net, it didn't really matter whether or not you had a permanent IP address. But now that you are setting up a Web site, you want to have a permanent IP address so people can find you! Your service provider will assign you a permanent address. Just ask.

Two Reasons You Might Park Your Page on Somewhere Else's Server

Reason 1: If you're short of funds, you may be able to park your Web pages on somebody else's Web server — usually your Internet provider's UNIX box — for a lot less money than any of the solutions in this chapter.

But what fun is that? Part of the joy of WebMastery is to have it there on your desk, to fiddle with endlessly until you get it right. Still, this may be the most practical thing to do until you can afford a full-time connection of your own. Talk to your provider about your options.

Reason 2: At the other end of the spectrum is the problem of having so much traffic on your site that your PC is overloaded or bandwidth becomes the bottleneck. We should all be so lucky. This means you've become successful! It also means you may have to move your Web pages to a faster UNIX box and turn the WebMaster role over to a UNIX system administrator to handle. (Or, of course, learn UNIX yourself …)

When the NASA space shuttle *Endeavor* home page was up, it had 600,000 hits over a five-day period. You can be sure it wasn't parked on a PC running Windows 3.1. You need to have a UNIX box and a T1 connection to handle that kind of traffic and not choke on it. Of course, if you run Windows NT or Linux on your box, that is a different matter and you should be able to handle some big-time traffic.

In the meantime, we hope this is a problem you encounter. It means you're a huge success and can pay a team of UNIX geeks to do it for you while you clip zero-coupon bonds.

OK. Now that that's out of the way, let's look at those aforementioned faster (and more expensive) connections.

ISDN and Other Digital Connections

There are a couple of ways to go if you decide to go for a dedicated digital connection instead of the analog modem route. They all work pretty much the same way as far as you are concerned: You've got a router hanging off your network connected to a terminal box. The terminal box in turn is connected to the line from your local phone. Your Internet provider's side of things is set up the same way in reverse. Sometimes they have a lot of money and a setup that can handle multiple types of digital and analog connections from different types of customers.

If you ever want to see every type of router, terminal server, and type of network and digital connectivity on Earth, go to the networking event of the year — Networld+Interop. The big one is held in the Spring in Vegas and is a blast. You'll get an unbelievable dose of media, protocols, Internet, infrastructure, network software, wireless/mobile, multimedia, and carrier/telecommunications. The show is one of the first ones ever to have a virtual trade show on the Web at **http:// www.interop.com.**

Whether you get a 56K line, ISDN, Frame Relay, fractional T1, or T1 (don't worry — all will be explained soon) is a matter of budget, your Internet provider's offerings, and your local phone company's technology. In some parts of the country the local phone companies are pushing Frame Relay, in others it's flat-rate ISDN. It depends on where you live.

We like ISDN. OK, we're biased. That's what we have. Southwestern Bell has a great deal on ISDN in Austin — installation is cheap (under $100) and we pay a flat rate of $50 a month. Your mileage may vary.

Because of its speed, reliability, and cost-effectiveness, many Internet providers are strongly committed to ISDN as the preferred method of connection for customers. In addition, the global Internet community is moving toward a standardized entry-level topology, and ISDN is rapidly emerging as the most universally accepted candidate.

Almost all Internet providers offer ISDN. There's a reason. ISDN operates at 64Kbps or 128Kbps, two to four times faster than a 28.8K modem's highest theoretical connect speed. ISDN is digital, therefore its bandwidth is guaranteed and error free. It's relatively easy to set up for both Internet providers and telephone companies.

If you decide on ISDN (or any other type of high-speed digital connection for that matter), get the advice of your Internet provider and telephone company before you do anything. Ask them what you need and how they recommend you go about getting it. You don't even need to know what ISDN stands for. ("Integrated Services Digital Network." There. Did that make you feel better? For what it's worth, many netizens say it stands for "I Still Don't Know.")

ISDN is nothing more than a digital telephone line. You get one by placing an order with your local phone company, assuming they offer ISDN service. Not all do. Yet. Be aware that there are different types of ISDN, ranging from ISDN on demand to bonded ISDN.

The one you care about is Basic Rate Interface ISDN or BRI. BRI is comprised of two "bearer" (B) 64K channels for user data plus one "data-link" (D) 16K channel for control and signaling information. Many Internet providers just set you up on one B channel, which gives you a 64Kbps connection to the Net — about two to four times faster than a 28.8K modem.

Here's where it gets interesting: You can "bond" the other 64K channel with the first to make a 128K connection. And you can just keep on bonding away with ISDN and end up with a PRI (Primary Rate Interface). PRI provides 23 data channels of 64Kbps each operating simultaneously and a 64Kbps signaling channel for communicating over an ISDN Primary Rate Service. By providing digital communication over twenty-three 64Kbps channels, many individual basic rate ISDN channels can be serviced over a single telephone company connection line. In North America and Japan, PRI consists of 24 channels, usually divided into 23 B channels and one D channel, and runs over the same physical interface as T1. Elsewhere it's 30 B channels and one D channel. Ask your Internet provider and your phone company; all you need is cash....

Monthly rates for a 64K dedicated ISDN connection vary widely. Just like the example of a dedicated modem connection, you're going to pay for both the phone line — in this case, it's a digital one — and for the connection to your Internet provider. Prices on ISDN and other types of digital connections vary widely depending on your location. There are promotional rates, flat rates, measured rates, "on-demand" rates, rates by byte usage, rates, rates, and more rates. You have to be a bean counter to compare offerings and rate packages and figure it all out. Look for something that's simple to understand, and as close to a flat rate as possible, from both the phone company and your service provider. Figure it's going to run you somewhere between $250 to $500 a month for a 64K ISDN connection by the time you're all done.

Ask your Internet provider how to get your ISDN line installed. They'll probably know a contact person at the local phone company who they have a good relationship with or at least took to lunch once.

One last thing: When you're going the ISDN route, it may be better to determine a budget, then leave it up to your Internet provider to tell you what to buy equipment-wise, and what speed connection you can get with that budget.

Typical Monthly Dedicated Rates

Here are the April 1995 rates for UUNET, (see coupon at the back of this book). You may not get as good a deal in your neck of the woods; you may do better. As always, your mileage may vary.

UUNET Price List AlterDial®
Dial-up SLIP or PPP Internet Access via High-Speed Modems

Metered Client Cost (3-month commitment required):
$30/month basic service fee, including 15 hours of local usage, Internet mail and USENET news for one user

$2.25/hour connection cost to local hub (after first 15 hours), $6/hour surcharge to 800 number (at all times)

$10/month optional charge for each additional POP e-mail account

$25 one-time start-up fee

Metered LAN Cost:
$49/month basic service fee

$3/hour connection cost to local hub, $9/hour to 800 number

$10/month optional charge each for Internet mail and USENET news via UUCP/TCP

$10/month optional charge for each POP account or $20 per concurrent NNTP session

$499 one-time start-up fee

Dedicated Cost:
$250/month service charge for unlimited use, including Internet mail and USENET news

$750 one-time start-up fee

Line costs are not included; please contact AlterNet Sales for pricing.

PHONE$HOME^SM (Telnet Only)

$2–$12/hour

UUCP Services (Internet Mail and USENET News)

Costs

$36 monthly account charge, $2.60–$16/hour connection charge

ISDN Workgroup^SM 64 Kbps or 128 Kbps Internet Service

For all standard features, including unlimited connect time:

Type of Charge	1 B Channels	2B Channels
Startup charge	$395	$495
Standard monthly charge	$295	$495
Monthly charge with 12-month commitment	$280	$475
Monthly charge with 24-month commitment	$265	$450

For additional options

POP accounts: $10 per month per mailbox

NNTP sessions: $10 per month per simultaneous session.

Equipment: Ascend Pipeline 50 ISDN Router: $1050 (when purchased with service)

56K Leased Line Internet Access

Costs

$795 one-time start-up fee

Monthly service fee: $695

Monthly service fee with 1-year term commitment[1]: $645

Monthly service fee with 2-year term commitment[1]: $595

$100/month optional charge for a USENET news feed and/or Internet mail via UUCP over TCP. There is no extra charge for Internet mail via SMTP.

56 Kbps Frame Relay Internet Access

$495 one-time start-up fee

Monthly service fee: $595

Monthly service fee with 1-year term commitment[1]: $545

Monthly service fee with 2-year term commitment[1]: $495

$100/month optional charge for a USENET news feed and/or Internet mail via UUCP over TCP. There is no extra charge for Internet mail via SMTP.

Fractional T-1 (128 Kbps) Frame Relay Internet Access*

$3,000 one-time start-up fee

Monthly service fee: $995

Monthly service fee with 1-year term commitment[1]: $895

*Available in selected service areas — please call for details.

---

1.   At the conclusion of the term, pricing will revert to the standard rates in effect. Any customer wishing to cancel service before the completion of the term will be required to pay 75% of the monthly charges for the months remaining on the contract.

T-1 Plus^{SM}

$5,000 one-time start-up fee

T-1 Usage Level	Burstable Service Monthly Rate	Fractional Service Monthly Rate
0 to 128 Kbps	$1,250	$1,100
128 Kbps to 256 Kbps	$1,750	$1,600
256 Kbps to 384 Kbps	$2,200	$2,050
384 Kbps to 512 Kbps	$2,500	$2,350
Over 512 Kbps	$3,000	N/A

T-1 Term Commitment

Discounted monthly rates with a 1-, 2-, or 3-year commitment. For a 1-year term, a 5% discount; for a 2-year term, a 10% discount; for a 3-year term, a 15% discount.

Optional 56K and T-1 equipment (available only with service):

Cisco 2501 router and 56K CSU/DSU	$1,895
Kentrox T-1 CSU/DSU	$1,325
Cisco 2501 router	$1,595
ATL 56K CSU/DSU	$365
Ascend 56K Pipeline LS56 with internal CSU/DSU	$1,325
Imatek 56K router with internal CSU/DSU	$995

10Plus®

$5,000 one-time start-up fee

Usage Level*	Monthly Usage Charge
0 to 128 Kbps	$1,500
128 Kbps to 256 Kbps	$2,000
256 Kbps to 512 Kbps	$2,500
Over 512 Kbps	$3,000

* Monthly charges based on typical usage level during the month.

Please call for availability and detailed pricing.

Line costs are not included in any service costs; please contact AlterNet Sales for pricing.

UUNET's Web Server Hosting Services

Standard (server connected via T-1 link)

One-time start-up fee: $400; Monthly charge (1st mo.): $300

Monthly charge, after first month:

MB of data retrieved	Monthly cost	Approximate maximum number of inquiries (per month)[a]
0–250	$300	2,000
251–500	$400	4,000
501–1000	$500	8,000
1001–1500	$600	12,000
1501–2500	$750	20,000

a. Approximate maximum number of inquiries per day based on a typical mix of text and graphical information on the server. Pages with extensive graphic or multimedia content will consume more bandwidth per inquiry. Please call for details.

Premium (server connected via 10 Mbps link)

One-time start-up fee: $850; Monthly charge (1st mo.): $900

Monthly charge, after first month:

MB of data retrieved	Monthly cost	Approximate maximum number of inquiries (per month)
0–2,500	$ 900	20,000
2,501–5,000	$1,200	40,000
5,001–10,000	$1,800	80,000
10,001–15,000	$2,300	125,000
15,001–20,000	$2,800	150,000
20,001–30,000	$3,600	250,000
30,001–40,000	$4,400	300,000
40,001 and up	$5,400	500,000 and up

SELECTING YOUR CONNECTION TYPE

There are several different kinds of local access options for physically connecting from your location to AlterNet, and beyond to the Internet. The connection type you select will depend on the type of services you are seeking and on the size of the user base you are trying to serve.

MAIL AND NEWS ACCESS ONLY

For occasional Internet users, who only wish to send and receive electronic mail and participate in special-interest newsgroup discussions, a dial-up UUCP connection is all that is needed.

INDIRECT IP ACCESS

A dial-up link to a provider's public-access machine, commonly dubbed a shell account. This account allows you to reach all Internet services that your provider makes available. However, some text and graphical applications, such as Mosaic, may not be used with a shell account. All files are stored on the provider's machine; you will need additional software to download them to your local computer.

FULL DIAL-UP IP ACCESS

Your computer becomes a official Internet host, with its own domain name, Internet address, and the ability to use the complete range of IP services with a standard modem. AlterNet's AlterDial® and ISDN Workgroup^{SM} dial-up services are perfect for users and organizations who want full Internet access without the expense of a full-time dedicated link.

FULL DEDICATED IP ACCESS

Full-time, full-service IP connectivity (mail, news, FTP, Telnet, Gopher, WAIS, WWW, Archie, Veronica, Mosaic, etc.) over a dedicated digital telephone line. Speeds range from 14.4 Kbps to T-1 (1.5 Mbps) and up. You choose the appropriate speed based on the number of users and the amount of traffic you expect

ALTERNET'S FAMILY OF PRODUCTS

PHONE$HOME is a cost-effective way to stay in touch while traveling. All across the continental US, you can dial in to one of our local-access numbers and work on your Internet hosts quickly and inexpensively.

AlterNet's UUCP services offer you reliable Internet mail and USENET news across the US and around the world. In addition to our mail and news services, UUCP offers proxy Internet file-transfer capabilities and access to our extensive on-line software and documentation archives.

AlterDial gives you direct TCP/IP access to the Internet and AlterNet's network. AlterDial provides unrestricted commercial access to Internet services such as mail, news, Telnet, FTP, Gopher, WAIS, Mosaic, the World Wide Web, and more. AlterDial customers can receive their own domain name and multiple POP mailboxes.

ISDN Workgroup service is designed for business LANs that need high-speed dialup access to the Internet. Connection speeds match those of digital leased lines (approximately four times faster than analog lines), at a cost which can be considerably lower.

56 Kbps service offers mid-sized businesses full access to the Internet, via either leased lines or Frame Relay technology. Frame Relay offers higher performance than "full-time" dialup access, at a lower cost than traditional leased-line solutions.

T-1 Plus is targeted towards subscribers with a variety of throughput requirements. You may choose from either the Burstable Service, which allows you to periodically "burst" up to the full 1.5 Mbps, or the Fractional Service, which permits speeds up to the upper limit of the tier you choose.

Our 10Plus service offers extremely high throughput Internet access to customers with demanding bandwidth requirements. Our 10 Mbps access offers the simplicity of a physical Ethernet interface, with prices usually associated with traditional T-1 access. You pay only for the bandwidth that you use on a sustained basis 95% of the month, as determined by traffic samples taken over our network every five minutes throughout the day.

UUNET'S WEB SERVER SERVICES

UUNET's Web server hosting services provide you with an easy and affordable way to establish and maintain your company's presence on the World Wide Web. You may choose from the Standard service, which places your information on a server connected to our 45 Mbps ATM backbone at T-1 (1.544 Mbps) speed; or the Premium service, in which your information is stored on a server connected to our backbone via a 10 Mbps link. Both options offer you 24-hour-a-day, 7-day-a-week monitoring; and reliable, fast access to your corporate information by anyone on the Internet. UUNET can also develop your Web server content, providing a fully-integrated service. Please call for details.

UUNET. The Internet Business Solution.

For more information, please contact:
UUNET Technologies, Inc.
3060 Williams Drive
Fairfax, Virginia 22031-4648 USA
+1 800 488 6383 (voice)
+1 703 206 5600 (voice)
+1 703 206 5601 (fax)
info@uu.net
http://www.uu.net

AlterNet, UUNET, AlterDial, and 10Plus are registered trademarks, and PHONE$HOME, T-1 Plus and ISDN Workgroup are service marks of UUNET Technologies, Inc. All other trademarks acknowledged.

For a Single PC (Not on a Network)

If your site is just a single PC that's not on a network, we like the IBM WaveRider ISDN card. It's priced at about $500 and from what we've looked at and heard from our service provider friends, the WaveRider seems to be the one that is most compatible with the different flavors of ISDN-capable boxes that Internet providers have at their end. But don't just run out and order one; as always, ask the advice of your service provider before you buy anything.

At the current prices for ISDN cards, you may be better off paying another $500 to $1000 and going with something like a Combinet box or a router from Ascend, which is what you use to set up a local-area network (LAN) on the Internet. Remember, as of this writing, an ISDN card will only allow one machine to be connected at a time. That leaves no room for growth if you decide later you'd like to add multiple Web servers or an FTP server, or if you want to use another PC to surf around the Net over that nice high-speed connection you're paying so dearly for.

For a LAN (Local-Area Network)

If you are on a LAN, your Internet provider will probably connect your network to theirs using a router box that works with ISDN. Go with their equipment recommendation. The cost at your end will run somewhere between $750 and $1500 for all the hardware, and another $50 to $150 a month for the ISDN line.

Your network administrator (that may be you, so pay attention) and Internet provider need to put their heads together and address the security issues that a LAN connection to the Net has the potential to create. There are issues you definitely need to consider. The main one of course, is that you don't want outside traffic to have access to your whole network. Your Internet provider can best recommend what "firewalls" can be put in place to restrict inbound access to your network to just the machine that is the Web server. They can also restrict outbound traffic for you so that other users on the LAN aren't just goofing off surfing the Net all day. If you are going to connect a LAN to the Internet you need to spend time looking at security issues that are beyond the scope of this book. You can learn more about the "firewall" world by reading *Firewalls and Internet Security* by William R. Cheswick and Steven M. Bellovin. It's published by Addison Wesley and goes for about $25. Firewalls are an arcane study in and of themselves.

What You Need to Know If You ARE Firewalled

Here's the deal. If the LAN you are on is "firewalled" from the Internet, get your network administrator and Internet provider to set your Web server up outside the firewall. Just remember, that makes it a sacrificial lamb. So don't keep company secrets on your Web server. And always, always have at least one backup of your entire server, so that you can restore it after a catastrophe.

There is a very big advantage to having your LAN connected to the Internet. Besides letting multiple users surf the Net over the same connection to the Internet, you can run multiple Web servers, FTP servers, and so on, all on different machines on your local network, and all connected to the Internet with one device.

If your LAN is already on the Net, just ask your network administrator to assign you a permanent IP address (and while you're at it, a host machine name for the PC you'll be using as a Web server) and you're in business!

Unless you are a serious telecommunications enthusiast or are the type who needs to know everything about everything before moving forward, leave the configuration of any digital connection to the Internet, such as ISDN, to your Internet provider and your local phone company. Let them have the joy of getting it all set up and running. It's their responsibility anyway. You can always come back when the dust settles and learn more.

By the way, an excellent resource on the Net for info on ISDN is at Dan Kegel's ISDN Page at **http://alumni.caltech.edu:80/~dank/isdn/**. Everything under the sun about ISDN is there. Knock yourself out.

IP Everywhere: Understanding Network Protocols

Besides the physical network or modem connection with your Internet provider, you need a permanent address on the Internet. (Remember a few pages ago we told you to get started on it ASAP?) If you don't already have one, it's time to get a domain name and IP address.

Getting Your Domain Name and Permanent IP Address

To be a Web site — or any other type of server on the Internet – you have to have a permanent IP address. You should also have a domain name, though strictly speaking, it's not mandatory. An IP address is a number — 204.96.111.158. A domain name is a name, like "outer.net" or "webmasterwin.com."

Because most humans don't deal well with numbers, the Internet uses names as "aliases" for the numbers. That way you can type the name of a site instead of trying to remember the number. You can, of course, use the IP number instead, but let's face it, **http://webmaster-win.com** is easier to remember than **http://204.96.111.154** for most people.

URLs

You know what URL stands for, right? If you've ever surfed, you've seen URLs. But sometimes you see something over and over but still aren't sure what it means.

URL stands for Universal Resource Locator. It's pronounced You-Are-Ell, not EARL. OK?

Web browsers navigate using URLs. You can always tell from the URL what type of site it is. For example, if the URL starts with "telnet://," as in **telnet://internic.net,** you can tell it's a Telnet site. If the URL starts with "ftp://," as in **ftp://gateway.dec.com,** it is an FTP site. If it starts with "http://," it's a Web server.

A Detour into DNS

The Internet keeps track of all the domain names and associated IP numbers with DNS, the Domain Name System. DNS was developed by Sun Microsystems in the early 1980s and is a vital part of the Internet. The World Wide Web is heavily dependent on a fully functioning Domain Name System. In a nutshell, DNS is a hierarchical distributed database system that lets Internet providers (also known as "hosts") keep track of IP addresses and host names in "Host Tables." The Host Table "resolves" a domain name into an IP number to be transmitted over the Internet.

Since there are so many IP addresses and domain names on the Internet, it's impractical for a provider's Host Table to keep a list of all of them. DNS deals with this by distributing the names up and over the net chain from host site to host site. This, coupled with a system of "lookups" when a host site or provider is unable to resolve a domain name into an IP number, makes the whole addressing scheme over the Internet function smoothly.

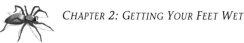

There's obviously more to how DNS actually works, but that should hold you. If you're really interested, you can talk about it over that lunch you are going to have with your service provider.

Before You Request ...

One thing you should do before requesting a domain name and IP number from your Internet provider is Telnet to the InterNIC and search the "Whois" database to see if the domain name you want is available. If you've never done this, here's how:

After making a connection to the Internet if necessary, Telnet to **internic.net**. When you get there you'll see a menu that looks like Figure 2.2.

You don't have to select anything from the choices presented. The prompt has you at the right place to begin. Just type the domain name you are interested in having to see if it is available, as shown in Figure 2.3.

Figure 2.2:   *The InterNIC "Whois" menu, January 1995.*

```
╔═══════════════════════════════ outer.net 1 ═══════════════════════════════╗
┃ *********************************************************************** ┃▲
┃ * -- InterNIC Registration Services Center  --                         ┃
┃ *                                                                      ┃
┃ * For gopher, type:              GOPHER <return> ** DISABLED **         ┃
┃ * For wais, type:                WAIS <search string> <return>         ┃
┃ * For the *original* whois type: WHOIS [search string] <return>        ┃
┃ * For referral whois type:       RWHOIS [search string] <return>       ┃
┃ *                                                                      ┃
┃ * For user assistance call (703) 742-4777 or (619) 455-4600            ┃
┃ # Questions/Updates on the whois database to HOSTMASTER@internic.net   ┃
┃ * Please report system problems to ACTION@internic.net                 ┃
┃ *********************************************************************** ┃
┃ Please be advised that use constitutes consent to monitoring           ┃
┃ (Elec Comm Priv Act, 18 USC 2701-2711)                                 ┃
┃                                                                        ┃
┃ 6/1/94                                                                 ┃
┃ We are offering an experimental distributed whois service called referral┃
┃ whois (RWhois). To find out more, look for RWhois documents, a sample   ┃
┃ client and server under:                                               ┃
┃ gopher: <rs.internic.net> InterNIC Registration Services ->            ┃
┃        InterNIC Registration Archives -> pub -> rwhois                 ┃
┃ anonymous ftp: <rs.internic.net> /pub/rwhois                           ┃
┃ Cmdinter Ver 1.3 Sat Jan 21 21:38:11 1995 EST                          ┃
┃ [vt100] InterNIC > █                                                   ┃▼
╚════════════════════════════════════════════════════════════════════════╝
```

Figure 2.3:   *The InterNIC "Whois" search, January 1995.*

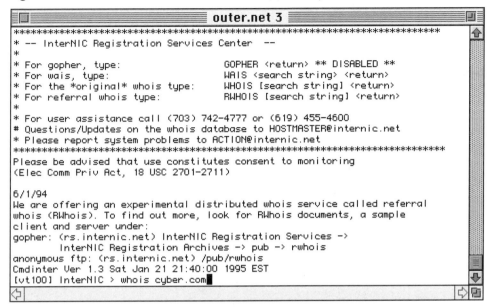

```
████████████████████ outer.net 3 ████████████████████
**********************************************************************
* -- InterNIC Registration Services Center  --
*
* For gopher, type:            GOPHER <return> ** DISABLED **
* For wais, type:              WAIS <search string> <return>
* For the *original* whois type:  WHOIS [search string] <return>
* For referral whois type:     RWHOIS [search string] <return>
*
* For user assistance call (703) 742-4777 or (619) 455-4600
# Questions/Updates on the whois database to HOSTMASTER@internic.net
* Please report system problems to ACTION@internic.net
**********************************************************************
Please be advised that use constitutes consent to monitoring
(Elec Comm Priv Act, 18 USC 2701-2711)

6/1/94
We are offering an experimental distributed whois service called referral
whois (RWhois). To find out more, look for RWhois documents, a sample
client and server under:
gopher: (rs.internic.net) InterNIC Registration Services ->
        InterNIC Registration Archives -> pub -> rwhois
anonymous ftp: (rs.internic.net) /pub/rwhois
Cmdinter Ver 1.3 Sat Jan 21 21:40:00 1995 EST
[vt100] InterNIC > whois cyber.com█
```

Figure 2.4:   *The InterNIC "Whois" results, January 1995.*

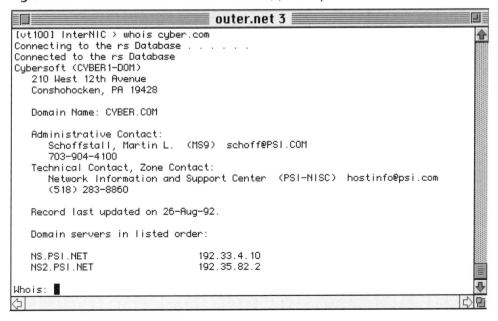

```
████████████████████ outer.net 3 ████████████████████
[vt100] InterNIC > whois cyber.com
Connecting to the rs Database . . . . . .
Connected to the rs Database
Cybersoft (CYBER1-DOM)
   210 West 12th Avenue
   Conshohocken, PA 19428

   Domain Name: CYBER.COM

   Administrative Contact:
      Schoffstall, Martin L.  (MS9)  schoff@PSI.COM
      703-904-4100
   Technical Contact, Zone Contact:
      Network Information and Support Center  (PSI-NISC)  hostinfo@psi.com
      (518) 283-8860

   Record last updated on 26-Aug-92.

   Domain servers in listed order:

   NS.PSI.NET                  192.33.4.10
   NS2.PSI.NET                 192.35.82.2

Whois: █
```

If you typed **cyber.com** you got back the information shown in Figure 2.4 on page 47.

Bummer. Try again — you need to be just a little more original. Remember that you're probably going to be a .com (pronounced "dot com"), which means you're a commercial organization. Here are some other common "dot" codes:

.edu = educational

.org = nonprofit organization

.net = Internet provider

.gov = government

.mil = millionaires (and military)

Once you've found a domain name you like that isn't already taken, call or eMail your Internet provider and get it registered. They should only charge you about $25 to $50 for this, if anything. Keep in mind that just because your search at the InterNIC didn't show that your domain name wasn't already taken, it doesn't guarantee that it's available. You're probably OK, but don't run off and spend money or time getting new business cards printed with that URL until you get a confirmation that the name is actually still available.

There is usually a big queue at the InterNIC. The name you like may be tucked in the queue somewhere and someone may get it before you. The last time we checked, the backlog at the InterNIC was over 3000 names, and the wait to get registered was over two weeks. (You can probably get it done sooner if your Internet provider is on a first-name basis with someone at the InterNIC.)

You can download the application from the InterNIC and apply yourself by going to the InterNIC registration services off the InterNIC Home Page at **http://www.internic.net**. But why bother? Your Internet provider has the same form and theirs is probably even easier to fill out. Unless they are charging extra to fill it out, have them do it; you've got enough work ahead of you. Do check out the InterNIC Home Page though. There's a ton of interesting Net info there.

What's the InterNIC?
Here's What "They" Say:

The InterNIC is a collaborative project of three organizations that work together to offer the Internet community a full scope of network information services. These services include providing information about accessing and using the Internet, assistance in locating resources on the network, and registering network components for Internet connectivity. The overall goal of the InterNIC is to make networking and networked information more easily accessible to researchers, educators, and the general public.

The InterNIC name signifies the cooperation between Network Information Centers, or NICs. The entire Internet community, in fact, is brimming with cooperative ventures, resource sharing, and collaborations. It is fitting, then, that the InterNIC is managed by three organizations operating under one umbrella.

General Atomics in San Diego, California, manages Information Services, providing the Scout Report, net happenings, NSF Network News, InterNIC, InfoGuide, InterNIC Briefcase, Reference Desk, seminars, and other services that respond to the needs of the scientific and education community.

Phone: +1-619-455-4600
Fax: +1-619-455-4640
eMail: refdesk@is.internic.net

AT&T in South Plainfield, New Jersey, manages Directory and Database Services, providing the Directory of Directories, Directory Services, Database Services and a help desk to assist both people making use of their services and additional support organizations who want to know more about offering these services to their own audiences.

Phone: +1-908-668-6587
Fax: +1-908-668-3763
eMail: admin@ds.internic.net

What's the InterNIC?
Here's What "They" Say: (continued)

Network Solutions, Inc., in Herndon, Virginia, manages Registration Services, providing Internet Protocol (IP) address allocation, domain registration, Autonomous System Number (ASN) assignment, and inverse addresses.

    Phone: +1-703-742-4777

    Fax: +1-703-742-4811

    eMail: hostmaster@rs.internic.net

For general information about the InterNIC, please send mail to info@internic.net.

Source: InterNIC Home Page **http://www.internic.net/**

Here's a nifty tip. You don't have to wait for your domain name to come through to turn on your Web site. Your Internet provider or network provider can give you a permanent IP number from their set, and then you can turn your Web site on for all the world to see (assuming you have your connection in place and something to show).

When the domain name finally comes through from the InterNIC, your provider will associate it with the IP number they gave you earlier,

---

How *Not* to Make Big Bucks ...

Do everyone a favor: Don't try to register domain names for big companies like Coke, McDonald's, or Circuit City. It won't fly, and they won't pay you big bucks for it someday.

The InterNIC is wise to this and they don't dig it. They can spot those bogus applications a mile away. Besides, don't you have any better ideas for your creativity? Knuckleheads who do these kinds of things on the Net are wasting bandwidth and making it take longer for anyone else to get a domain name. Besides, that kind of stuff will almost certainly get you mailbombed by the UNIX cybergods if they find out.

put it in their Host Table, and it will automatically get distributed through the entire DNS system of the Internet in the course of a few days. (See! Now you know why we included that seemingly incongruous section on DNS a few pages back.)

If you are part of an organization that already has a domain name set up, you can contact your network administrator or Internet provider and obtain a host name (as well as an IP number) for the PC you will be using as a Web server. That would be everything you need — you lucky dog. If you're in this boat, you can make your request for a permanent IP number and host name for your machine in a single call.

Now What?

Assuming you're connected, took our tip, went ahead and got a permanent IP number and have put in your application for a domain name ASAP as we suggested, what do you do next? Learn to set up a Web server, of course!

WebServer: A First Look

Now we're going to show you how to get WebServer up and running and be a network of one — and you don't even need a connection to the Internet. If you already have a dial-up SLIP or PPP account, we'll even show you what you can do with the IP number off your TCP/IP stack, the one we told you about before that is assigned automatically by your Internet provider during a connection. With that number, you can be a Web site on the Net, at least for as long as your current connection remains open. Of course, no one will know unless you call them up, tell them the IP number, and tell them to point their browser at that IP address. This Web site won't have a domain name yet, and if you end this connection, when you reconnect you may not have the same IP number. But you can definitely call your friends and have them check out your site with their Web browser.

But that's just an added thrill. This section is designed to put you ahead of the game, so that when you've got your dedicated connection

and permanent IP and domain name, you'll have some idea of what it takes to get a Web site up and running.

WebServer: Your First Time

It's time to jump in and fire up Quarterdeck's WebServer. Make sure you are *not* connected to the Internet for this, at least for now. The approach we're going to take is to just build a Web page quickly. We'll go back and tweak it and add the bells and whistles and show you how to "turn it on" for the general public in upcoming chapters.

At the end of this tutorial, you'll have set up your PC as a WWW server. OK, here's what you need:

System Requirements

To set up your PC as a WWW site you'll need the following:

- At least 8 megs of RAM
- At least 4 megs free disk space
- Windows 3.1
- A 486/33 PC or better
- A SLIP, PPP, or dedicated connection to the Internet
- Winsock 1.1-compliant network stack

Before we march ahead and help you set up your PC as a WWW server, you've got to let us make a couple of assumptions about where you're at already, OK? Here's the big one. We assume you have had at least a SLIP or PPP account with an Internet provider working properly. We also assume that if your PC is part of an Ethernet LAN that you have got the Net connection thing down. OK. We admit it. That may seem like a lot to ask. Well, we have to draw the line somewhere. There are so many different TCP/IP stacks, Ethernet cards, drivers, and Net apps for the PC, that going over all of them would be impossible. The whole thing is voodoo anyway. We figure you already slugged this stuff out to get this far. Fair assumption, right? Good.

Here's the deal though — and it may upset your apple cart, so get ready.

Thanks to Quarterdeck

We worked closely with Quarterdeck to make sure you have everything you need to get up and going with the version of WebServer included on the CD-ROM. They even gave us permission to include many sections of their user guide in the pages following.

Six Steps to Setting Up WebServer

Here is a quick overview of the steps required to install WebServer.

1. Run the installation program, INSTALL.EXE, off the CD. If the Install program modifies your AUTOEXEC.BAT file, reboot your computer after the installation is finished.

2. Run WebServer by double-clicking on its icon. WebServer should run properly without any additional configuration, but if the icon does not appear, look at C:\HTTPD\HTTPD.LOG (the default file name) for an explanation.

3. Test WebServer by running your Web browser and typing the following URL:

   ```
   http://yourservername/
   ```

If WebServer and your Winsock are working together properly, you will see the default home page display on the browser's screen.

4. On the default home page, click on "Server Demonstration" in the "Getting Started" section to test WebServer's features.

5. After WebServer has been tested, replace the Quarterdeck home page with your own (if you used all the defaults when installing WebServer, the filename for your home page is C:\HTTPD\HTDOCS\INDEX.HTM). Don't worry if you don't already have a home page; you'll learn how to make one in the next chapter.

The installation program automatically creates a backup of the Web-Server sample home page as INDEX.SAV that you can use for reference as you edit the actual .HTM file.

6. Test WebServer on the network (whether LAN or Internet) by connecting the server computer to the Internet or LAN, running WebServer, and trying to access your server's home page from another machine on the same network. On the other machine, use the same URL (with your IP address or host name) you used in step 3, above. Contact your Internet service provider or network system administrator for more information on connecting to the Internet or to a LAN.

Installing Quarterdeck WebServer

During the installation, you will be asked whether you want to install LAN WorkPlace, a software package that contains the network support programs (called the "network stack") needed to run Quarterdeck Web-Server. Different network environments require different network stacks; some network packages rely upon custom features built into particular network stacks. LAN WorkPlace has a general-purpose network stack that works with a range of network adapters in several different network environments. If your network operations depend on custom functions in your network stack, you may not want to install the LAN WorkPlace stack; if you are unsatisfied with your current stack, you might like to try the LAN WorkPlace stack. Your Internet service provider or network manager can provide you with precise technical details on the requirements of your particular network environment, but here are our general recommendations:

- If you have no network software at all, or if your software will not support WebServer, you *must* install LAN WorkPlace to provide the network files necessary to run WebServer.

- If you already have network software that is necessary to operate some function in your current network, or are a SLIP or PPP user, we recommend that you do *not* install LAN WorkPlace unless you are having trouble with your current network stack or if you discover that your network stack cannot support WebServer.

The instructions below assume you are installing Quarterdeck WebServer from CD drive J to hard drive C. If you are using other disk drives, please make the appropriate substitutions.

1. Start Windows.
2. Put the WebMaster Windows CD into your drive.
3. Pull down the Program Manager's File menu and select **Run**.
4. Type **J:INSTALL** and click **OK**.

   You will see an information screen summarizing installation requirements (Figure 2.5).

Figure 2.5: *Installation requirements screen.*

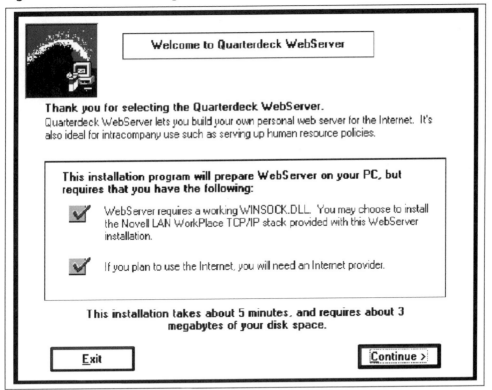

5. Click **Continue**.

What happens next depends upon whether you already have Winsock-compliant TCP/IP software installed on your system.

- If you see the message **No Network Detected**, the Installation program did not detect any network software with a satisfactory TCP/IP layer or Winsock-compliant interface (or any network whatsoever). In this case, the **Install LAN WorkPlace** box will be checked automatically because WebServer requires this network software.

- If you see a dialog box titled **Active WINSOCK Detected**, the Installation program has detected an active Winsock-compliant TCP/IP interface, but this may or may not meet WebServer's requirements (WebServer requires a version 1.1-compliant Winsock). If you see the **Active WINSOCK Detected** message and you do not want to replace your existing stack, *do not* check the **Install LAN WorkPlace** box. If you subsequently have problems, you can reinstall LAN WorkPlace from the CD-ROM, but you must completely *uninstall* the old stack before installing LAN WorkPlace. Note: We recommend that SLIP and PPP users should *not* install LAN WorkPlace unless you have trouble using your existing Winsock.

6. Click **Continue** to proceed.

   A dialog box for user information displays (Figure 2.6).

Figure 2.6: *Dialog box for user information.*

Personalize Your Quarterdeck Product.

Please complete the following information. Correct information will be required by Quarterdeck Technical Support.

Name:

Company: Quarterdeck Corporation

City: Santa Monica   State: CA

Country: USA

Your serial number is located on your product diskette.

Serial Number:

Exit   Continue >

7. Fill out the fields in this dialog box. Click **Continue** to proceed.

The Installation Options dialog box displays (Figure 2.7).

Figure 2.7: *WebServer Installation Options dialog box.*

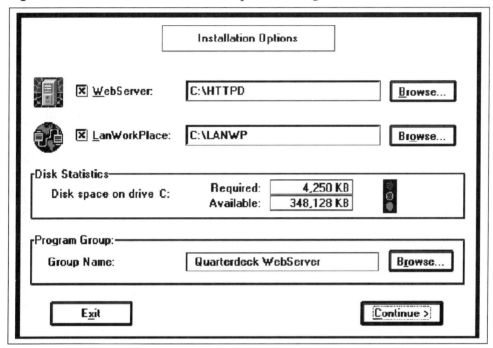

In the middle of the dialog box is a **Disk Statistics** panel listing the disk space required and the disk space available. If you do not have enough disk space to install WebServer, click **Exit**, and free up the required amount of space.

8. At the top of the dialog box is a **WebServer** check box and a text box for the WebServer pathname. To install WebServer, be sure the **WebServer** box is checked. You can use the text box to change the default installation directory. If you need to change the pathname, you can enter it directly in the text box, or you can use the **Browse** button to assist entering the pathname.

9. Near the top of the dialog box is a **LAN WorkPlace** check box and a text box for the LAN WorkPlace pathname. To install LAN Work-

Place, be sure the **LAN WorkPlace** box is checked. You can use the text box to change the default installation directory. If you need to change the pathname, you can enter it directly in the text box, or you can use the **Browse** button to assist entering the pathname.

10. At the bottom of the dialog box is a **Program Group** panel. If you want to change the program group into which you will install Quarterdeck WebServer, click the **Browse** button and select the appropriate program group.

11. Click **Continue**.

12. If you are installing WebServer for the first time, skip this step and proceed to step 13.

   If you are upgrading an existing WebServer installation, you will be prompted whether to overwrite your existing configuration files or sample HTML files. Check the appropriate boxes if you want to upgrade those files. The Installation User Options dialog box displays (Figure 2.8).

Figure 2.8: *Installation User Options dialog box.*

```
┌─────────────────────────────────────────────────────────┐
│  ┌─────────────────────────────────────────────────┐    │
│  │          ┌──────────────────────────────┐       │    │
│  │          │    Installation User Options  │       │    │
│  │          └──────────────────────────────┘       │    │
│  │                                                  │    │
│  │   Please provide the following information for the WebServer installation. │
│  │                                                  │    │
│  │   ┌User Information─────────────────────────┐   │    │
│  │   │                                          │   │    │
│  │   │   ▨   E-mail address:  ┌──────────────┐ │   │    │
│  │   │                        │              │ │   │    │
│  │   │                        └──────────────┘ │   │    │
│  │   └──────────────────────────────────────────┘   │    │
│  │                                                  │    │
│  │   ┌Location Information─────────────────────┐   │    │
│  │   │   🌐  Time Zone:  ┌─────────────────┐ ▣ │   │    │
│  │   │                   │Los Angeles, CA, USA [GMT-08:00]│ │
│  │   │                   └─────────────────┘    │   │    │
│  │   │              ☐ Sort by TimeZone          │   │    │
│  │   └──────────────────────────────────────────┘   │    │
│  │                                                  │    │
│  │   ┌──────┐          ┌────────┐ ┌─────────────┐  │    │
│  │   │ Exit │          │ < Back │ │ Start Install│  │    │
│  │   └──────┘          └────────┘ └─────────────┘  │    │
│  └─────────────────────────────────────────────────┘    │
└─────────────────────────────────────────────────────────┘
```

13. In the first text box, enter the e-mail address of the server's administrator. This address will automatically be included on server error messages so that users receiving those messages know who to contact regarding server problems. The address should be a valid e-mail address for your site. Consult your network manager or Internet service provider if you need more information about e-mail addresses.

    In the second box, select your time zone.

14. Click **Start Install**. Quarterdeck WebServer will now be installed on your hard drive. When you are asked to do so, insert any additional installation disk(s).

    As the installation progresses, you may see questions regarding changes to AUTOEXEC.BAT or Windows configuration files. We recommend that you allow the installation program to make the suggested changes. Follow the on-screen instructions and answer the prompts appropriately.

If you are not installing LAN WorkPlace, we're done with the installation of the Quarterdeck WebServer, and you're ready to rock. If you need to install a network TCP/IP stack, go ahead and run through the LAN WorkPlace setup screens.

Starting Quarterdeck WebServer

To start WebServer, double-click the Quarterdeck WebServer icon in the Quarterdeck WebServer program group.

- When you start Quarterdeck WebServer, you will see the WebServer window display briefly. Then, WebServer will minimize automatically to an icon at the bottom of the Windows desktop. If the server does not start successfully—that is, the server icon does not appear on the desktop or in the task list—look in C:\HTTPD\HTTPD.LOG (the default filename) for an explanation. And if that doesn't help, you're hosed. Go ahead and call their tech support at 310-392-9701.

Shutting Down Quarterdeck WebServer

To shut down Quarterdeck WebServer:

1. Maximize the WebServer icon.
2. Select one of two ways to shut down the server:

   For a more graceful shutdown, pull down the File menu and select **Exit**. Quarterdeck WebServer will wait for any currently active network requests to conclude, then will shut down and exit, or for an immediate shutdown, pull down the File menu and select **Force Exit**. Quarterdeck WebServer will immediately terminate any active network requests, then shut down and exit.

Testing the Server

After installing your server, you should test it. To test WebServer,

1. Start WebServer.
2. Run a Web browser like Quarterdeck Mosaic.
3. Display your home page with this URL:

```
http://yourhost/
```

replacing "yourhost" with your server's host name or IP address. If you are unsure of your host name or IP address, see your network manager or Internet service provider.

You must use your server's IP address or host name to display the home page if you want to test WebServer. If you use your browser's "local" mode, you will bypass WebServer, and some of the test documents that use server functions will not operate properly.

If you want to test the server without being connected to the Internet or a network, you may be able to use the loopback IP address: 127.0.0.1 (on some systems, this number is also assigned the name "localhost"). If your Windows socket driver has a host table, check to see if "localhost" is already there. If it is not, add it, and you will be able to test the server without being connected to the Internet or a network. Note: the loopback address is defined by your Winsock package. Not all Winsocks support this feature.

4. When you display the server's home page, you should see a link on the home page to "server demonstration." Click on this link to verify your server's installation. You will see links to the following topics:

    –Basic document retrieval

    –Document-based queries

    –Form-based queries and submissions

    –Directory-tree navigation and file retrieval

    –Imagemaps (graphic images with "clickable" hotspots)

    –Windows CGI

It will only take a few minutes to go through each of these sections, but it is important to work through each of the tests. You can also learn a lot about how Quarterdeck WebServer works by examining the test documents themselves (to view a document's HTML code in your browser, use its "document source" command).

Congratulations All Around!

You are now your own Web site on a TCP/IP network of one. Pretty easy, huh? Feel like you missed something? You didn't. It's just that simple. Try that on a UNIX server! Ha!

What you are looking at is a sample WebServer home page. All the hypertext you can wind your way through from there is the basis for a lot of the book. After all, we didn't invent anything here. You know the phrase — "there's nothing new under the sun."

Now don't run off shooting eMail to everyone you know and posting the location of your WWW site all over the Net. At least not yet. To start with, you're not connected to the Net. Further, you don't have a permanent IP address configured that works outside your little world. In other words, you still have a few housekeeping chores to do. But it was

time to get your Web site up and running, and with those last few steps, you've done just that. Give yourself a hand.

A Final Note About the TCP/IP Stack

We sincerely hope you are one of the lucky souls on Earth who gets everything right the first time around — or who has the patience of Job to hang in there. Once you have the IP part in place, the rest is a cakewalk.

We found that the most difficult thing in the whole setup we just described was the item we glossed over and assumed you already had in place — a connection to the Net. It is way, way, way easier to get a Web server up and running serving your Web pages than it is to get your SLIP or PPP and TCP/IP stack working properly on a PC with Windows. Even more trying is to get an Ethernet card installed and configured to handle IP traffic over a network with multiple protocols running over the same cable (IPX and TCP/IP for instance). It ain't plug and play — no way, no how, no ifs, ands, or buts about it.

The best recommendation we can make is to be persistent with your Internet provider or your network administrator, and, if need be, the manufacturer of your Ethernet card. There are so many nuances and combinations of cards and drivers — someone should write a really big, fat book.

It won't be either of us.

What You Just Installed

Installing WebServer was easy. You simply chose the directory for the server, supplied your e-mail address, told the server what time zone you were in, and you were ready to rock. Behind the scenes, the server creates a directory structure and installs all the server's essential binary and data files. It also sets two system variables: "TZ" in your AUTOEXEC.BAT file, which tells the server your time zone, and "CommandEnvSize" in your SYSTEM.INI file, which increases your DOS virtual machine environment (necessary for DOS-based CGI scripts)

The installation program installs the WebServer software itself, plus a number of support files in several different subdirectories.

Table 2.1: *WebServer directory structure*

Directory	Purpose
\HTTPD	The default root directory for Quarterdeck WebServer (also holds the server program itself). Also called the *server root directory*.
\HTTPD\CONF	Contains configuration files
\HTTPD\ICONS	Contains icons used in directory lists
\HTTPD\HTDOCS	Parent directory for HTML documents (also contains sample documents); also called the *document root directory*
\HTTPD\LOGS	Contains the server's transaction log files

Also under the \HTTPD "server root directory" are several subdirectories reserved only for "scripts"—custom applications which clients can run remotely. The "CGI" in the directory names refers to the "Common Gateway Interface" that the server uses with scripts. Hold that thought—we'll get to those later. But here's what the WebServer script directories look like.

Table 2.2: *WebServer script directories*

Script Directory	Purpose
\HTTPD\CGI-BIN\DOS	Contains executables for DOS-based scripts (including .BAT files)
\HTTPD\CGI-BIN\WINDOWS	Contains executables for Windows-based scripts
\HTTPD\CGI-SRC\DOS	Contains source code for DOS-based scripts
\HTTPD\CGI-SRC\WINDOWS	Contains source code for Windows-based scripts

Get Help If You Need It

If at any time you're completely fried and don't know what the heck is going on, Quarterdeck has fabulous online help.

To view Quarterdeck WebServer's online help do any of the following:

- Double-click the **Quarterdeck WebServer Help** icon in the Quarterdeck WebServer program group.
- From the WebServer setup utility, press **F1** or click the on-screen **Help** button.
- From the WebServer server window, use the pull-down **Help** menu, or press **F1**.

To view WebServer HTML document files:

1. Start WebServer.

   Use a web browser (such as Quarterdeck Mosaic) to open the WebServer home page, using this URL:

   ```
   http://yourhost/
   ```

   substituting **"yourhost"** with your server's name or IP address.

2. Follow the hypertext links to the server documentation.

You can view the home page in "local mode" without using the server's network capabilities by opening the file C:\HTTPD\HTDOCS\INDEX. HTM. However, "local mode" bypasses WebServer, and server test documents that require server functions will not operate correctly.

Everything You Need to Know About Client–Server Architecture

We almost forgot. We promised an overview of the client–server thing. Let's recap: You have your Web server up, even if you're just a "network of one" for now. That was no big deal, right? In fact, it was easy. So now we'll step back and take a bird's-eye look at what we've done so far.

You've got your TCP/IP stack, your WebServer, and your Web browser of choice all humming along perfectly. Let's finish with a bang, with a diagram that explains these elements and brings the whole client–server story into focus (Figure 2.5). Why are we doing this? Because they say a picture is worth a thousand words and neither of us feels like writing another thousand words about something as boring as client–server architecture.

Figure 2.9: *The client–server story.*

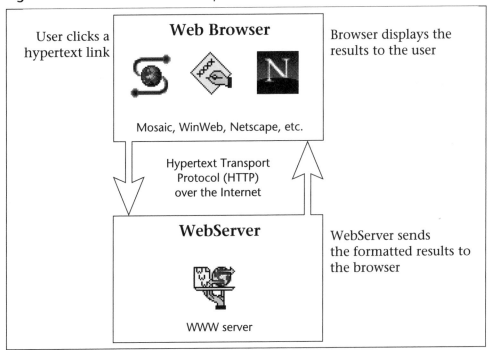

Wrap It Up

It's a wrap. You've now learned all you need to know about getting connected. Don't forget our most important advice: Go with what your Internet provider recommends given your budget.

You now know how to set up WebServer. That's enough left-hemisphere behavior for one sitting.

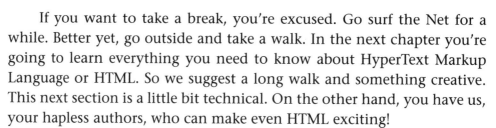

If you want to take a break, you're excused. Go surf the Net for a while. Better yet, go outside and take a walk. In the next chapter you're going to learn everything you need to know about HyperText Markup Language or HTML. So we suggest a long walk and something creative. This next section is a little bit technical. On the other hand, you have us, your hapless authors, who can make even HTML exciting!

So take that break, then turn the page.

Chapter 3

Introduction to HTML

*HTML: Not Just an Acronym for
"How to Make Levitusburgers" Anymore*

OK — let's face the music. In order to serve up pages, text, graphics, and everything else on your Web server, you're going to have to learn some HTML (HyperText Markup Language). It's not rocket science—in fact, it's not bad at all as languages go; ever program in PostScript? That means it's not going to take hundreds of pages to explain. All we ask from you is that you learn a few rules. Soon, you'll be an expert just like we are. <grin>

Introducing HTML...You're Gonna Love It

Learning HTML is going to be a little like going back to the early days of word processing when you had to type "bold" before and after the word you wanted to be bold.

Lovely, eh?

Until someone comes out with a great HTML editor that does it all and treats all your pages as one big integrated document — more along the lines of PageMaker, QuarkXPress or FrameMaker — you're just going to have to labor with typing out HTML codes. As we are writing this, the best and easiest way to create HTML code is to use SoftQuad's HoTMetaL Pro (more on this later). FrameMaker and Word have HTML filters that look promising but were unavailable for testing. By the time you read this, we hope you'll be able to take advantage of *the* killer HTML editor. Until then, you're going to have to tough it out, learn the markup elements of HTML, and obey the HTML cybergods.

What Makes HTML Worth the Hassle?

HTML is a subset of SGML (Standard Generalized Markup Language), which is a subset of ancient Greek. (We're just kidding, but mark our words, all these acronyms are eventually going to ruin some crossword puzzler's Sunday morning.) For all of its kludgy-ness and programmer's code-like look, HTML is actually a pretty nifty authoring language for WWW. In a nutshell, it's what allows the same Web pages to be viewed by a PC, a Mac, an Amiga, or even a UNIX box. That's very cool.

An HTML document consists of text, formatting, defined hypertext links, and anchors, and adheres to a strict set of document formatting rules. Stick with us and you'll learn them all.

When you create a page with HTML, you don't specify whether the title of a document should be displayed in a particular font such as Times Roman with a point size of 14. Instead, you use HTML code to instruct the browser how to display your page's parts — its title, text, images, and so on. It's left entirely to the user's browser — Netscape, Mosaic, or whatever — to recognize HTML tags and attributes and display the pages.

The defaults and/or preferences set in the client's browser determine how things are going to look. So relax, don't worry, and try to do your HTML right. Everything else is up to the browser.

Most people don't bother or even know that they can change the style preferences in their Web browser and do all sorts of wild-looking things with your boring old HTML. For that matter, most users never change the default URL to something other than the NCSA Home Page or Netscape Communications.

Rest assured. If you use proper HTML markup codes, your pages will look great in any browser on any platform.

HTML: The Good, the Bad, and the Ugly

HTML makes life simple. Imagine what it would be like if you had to do a separate Web page for every type and version of Web browser out there — each one with its own defaults and preferences for displaying HTML. You'd be up all night for a month of Sundays.

On the other hand, HTML limits what you can do creatively with formatting, leaving your page wide open for users to wreak havoc on by specifying weird fonts and things in their Web browser's preferences. (Though, as we said before, most don't.)

Like everything in life, there is Good, Bad, and Ugly when you write HTML code. What's Good is that HTML makes it possible for PC, Mac, and UNIX users to all see each other's stuff with a nice graphical, hypertext interface. It's the Esperanto that never was — or something like that.

The Bad is that it's still kind of geeky and requires a certain amount of concentration to get right.

The Ugly? Surf the Web for five minutes and we promise you'll come across examples of Ugly.

Steal This HTML

One of the best ways to learn HTML is to take a look at other people's HTML by choosing to view the source with your Web browser. It's OK to beg, borrow, and steal, but don't forget to thank the WebMasters whose source HTML you use. You should know that there is a slight pitfall to nabbing HTML and modifying it to suit your purposes: Not every Web-Master adheres to the accepted HTML standards. (We're sticklers for accurate HTML formatting, so stick with us and we'll teach you how to do it right.)

When you see HTML that looks clean, it's obvious that the WebMaster cared about the work he or she did. We like seeing HTML where all the markup code is in uppercase (or all in lowercase — just as long as it's

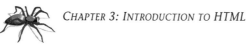

consistent). We like seeing HTML where the layout is easy to follow and care was taken with line wrapping.

Unfortunately, a lot of the HTML we've seen is sloppy. When you are looking at other people's source HTML, take a look at large commercial sites, where the HTML code is more likely to adhere to the guidelines. Some of the best work out there is the stuff done by the HTML troops of the O'Reilly Global Network Navigator site. We recommend you at least take a peek at their HTML source at **http://www. gnn.com**. That's what good HTML should look like.

Since Web browsers are becoming increasing particular about what they recognize as correct HTML, it is becoming more and more important to adhere to standard HTML. That's what we'll show you in this chapter. (And, of course, you can always get the *latest* version of HTML standards from the WebMaster Win server at **http://www.webmaster-win. com**.)

HTML QuickStart

All you need to get started creating HTML is any text editor. You can even use Microsoft Word. Just remember to save your documents as text files. We both like SoftQuad's HoTMetaL Pro. It runs about $195 (there's a link to a free demo version of it on the WebMaster Windows WWW server). Try it out.

HoTMetaL Pro has a great set of features that makes creating HTML a blast — at least compared to what it used to be when your only option was to type everything out. It forces you to stay within accepted HTML conventions too. You can just type out some plain text, select the HTML Markup Tag from the menu bar and, blammo, instant HTML. You can grab the free version of HoTMetaL Pro at: **ftp://ftp.cs.concordia.ca/ pub/www/Tools/Editors/SoftQuad/hot-metal**

Do that now, launch it, and we'll take a look at what HTML looks like (Figure 3.1).

If this is the first time you've looked closely at HTML, don't flip out. You'll get over it. We did. The best thing you can do to learn HTML is, as the Nike commercials say, "Just Do It."

Figure 3.1: *Sample HTML Home Page (text).*

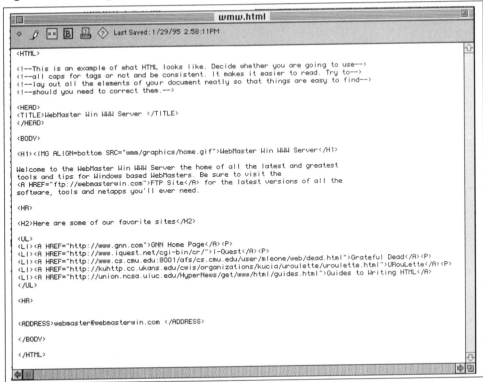

Go ahead and type everything you see in Figure 3.1. You can leave out the lines that begin with **<!** if you're a lousy typist. Those are called *comment lines* and won't appear to a Web browser unless a user views your source HTML. They're used to make notes to yourself in your HTML document. Start each line of comment with **<!** and end it with **>**. (You just learned how to code a comment line in HTML. That wasn't so bad, was it?)

After you've typed out or copied over all that HTML, save the file as **wmm.html.*** Now fire up your Web browser (you don't have to be on the Net to do this) and open the file named **wmm.html**. It should look something like Figure 3.2 on page 72 (our browser-of-choice is Netscape, by the way).

---

* If you're not running Windows 95 yet, save your file as .htm.

Figure 3.2:   *HTML code from Figure 3.1 viewed with a browser (Netscape).*

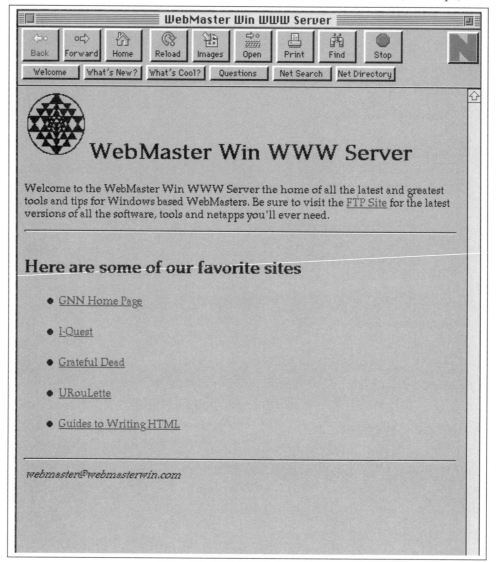

Whenever you are coding HTML, it's a good idea to have your Web browser open to check your work. In fact, it's a good idea to take a look at your HTML with *as many popular browsers as you can.* Take a look at it on a PC, a Mac, and on a UNIX machine if possible.

OK. That's a quick look at creating HTML code and then viewing it. Now let's get serious …

Tags (You're It)

There are three main components to HTML: tags, attributes, and URLs. By way of general definition:

- Tags tell the Web browser how to display text.
- Attributes tell the tag what action to take and are different depending on the tag with which they are associated.
- URLs are used to specify the location of linked files and indicate the type and address of the resource being accessed (e.g., WWW, Gopher, WAIS, FTP, etc.).

In this section we'll talk about tags — technical tags, formatting and styling tags, and even logical tags. Mostly, tags tell the browser how to display your words (and pictures, but we'll do pictures a little later).

There are all sorts of tags. Tags usually come in pairs and are bracketed by the < (less than) and > (greater than) signs. Of the pair, one tag starts the action and the other ends it. For instance, take the line:

```
<TITLE>WebMaster Windows WWW Server </TITLE>
```

You spotted the set of tags, right? **<TITLE>** and **</TITLE>**.

Just in Case: Upper, Lower, or Mixed Case?

Tags aren't case sensitive. You could just as easily use **<title>** and **</title>**. We recommend you use uppercase, however; we think it makes tags easier to identify and the fact of the matter is that you'll be following accepted HTML standards. Most plug-ins and HTML editors we've seen are also doing it that way.

Those Wild, Wacky Technical Tags

There are a couple of basic markup tags that every HTML document has that have nothing to do with how the contents of the Web page are displayed. These tags are ones that give important information to the browser.

The HTML Tag

The first such tag is the document identifier tag, **<HTML>** and **</HTML>**. This tag tells the Web browser that the document is an HTML document. Everything else that goes to make up a Web page is nested inside this tag. Some browsers don't require that you have the **<HTML>** **</HTML>** tag in your Web page. Pretend they do. It will probably be important in the future. Quite a bit of HTML markup is like this: It doesn't matter now but it might in the future. There are also a bunch of ways you can use different tags to make the browser display your HTML the same way. We're only going to show you the way that works and is the right way, not the way that just works.

The HEAD and TITLE Tags

Every HTML document should also have a Title tag, **<HEAD>** and **</HEAD>**. You can put some comments in the header if you want using the <! and > tags. Other than that, the only thing that usually goes between **<HEAD>** **</HEAD>** is the Title tag, **<TITLE>** and **</TITLE>**. The title (and head) is used for document identification. It is what appears in a browser's title, its hot list, and when View History is selected. There should only be one Title tag per document. Choose a descriptive title; one that is short and to the point.

Right:

```
<TITLE>WebMaster Windows WWW Server</TITLE>
```

Wrong:

```
<TITLE>My Home Page</TITLE>
```

And keep it as short as you can; depending on the browser, a long title may get truncated when displayed in hot lists and menu items like View History.

The BODY Tag

The fourth type of technical tag that gives information to the browser and doesn't affect the content of your document is the **<BODY> </BODY>** tag. It's another tag that isn't required by most browsers to do their thing ... yet. This tag indicates the beginning and end of the document contents you are going to be serving up.

Technical Tag Recap

Here are the pieces of an HTML document that we have learned so far; you should consider all except the comment tag — <! > — to be required.

```
<HTML>
<! >
<HEAD>
<TITLE> </TITLE>
</HEAD>
        <BODY>
      </BODY>
</HTML>
```

Formatting and Style Tags

Are you beginning to get a feel for how formal HTML is? You better have interesting content, because it ain't gonna be the HTML that keeps people coming back for more. There *are* a few things you can do with HTML to dress up your pages and play with the visuals, but not many.

Heading Tags

Heading tags are written with the format **<H1>** and **</H1>** and are of types H1 to H6 with descending font size and emphasis for each type. It is completely up to the browser's configuration as to how an H1 header, an H2 header, and so on look. Generally H1 will be seen as the largest, boldest text, H2 somewhat smaller, and so on. Try to use heading tags, at least two or three levels deep, to organize your documents.

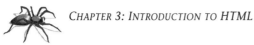

Let's take a look at Figures 3.1 and 3.2 again. Do you see the HTML line that begins with **<H1>** and ends with **</H1>**? (Ignore the IMG ALIGN stuff for a sec — that's an attribute; we'll cover them in full in a few pages.) Find the line in Figure 3.1 that begins with **<H2>**. Now take a look at Figure 3.2 and see how that line appears in our browser.

By the way, it's not uncommon for the text that appears between the **<H1>** and **</H1>** the first time to be the same as that which appears between **<TITLE>** and **</TITLE>.** It may even be a good idea to do it this way. You decide.

OK, so that's the story on the header markup stuff. It's kind of like an outline. Play around with it a bit if you like, creating some text with each of the tags, **<H1>** and **</H1>**, **<H2>** and **</H2>**, and so on. You'll see that it's pretty straightforward.

The Paragraph, Line Break, and Rule Tags

Two things browsers don't care about when they see an HTML document are white space and carriage returns. If you want to separate paragraphs of text, use the Paragraph tag, **<P>.** Put it at the beginning or end of the text you would like to separate as a distinct paragraph.

If what you want is a line break, not a new paragraph, use the Line Break tag, **
.**

One more quickie and then we'll show you another example that includes most of what you know so far.

If you want to have a line under some text or use a line to separate text you use the Rules tag, **<HR>.** The **<HR>** tag also causes a paragraph break. Keep that in mind when you are using it.

The **<P>**, **
,** and **<HR>** tags don't require the corresponding ending tags of **</P>, </BR>,** and **</HR>.**

We're starting to see **</P>** being used at the beginning and at the end of a paragraph; this usage forms a "container" of text in HTML+, the successor to HTML. This is yet another one of those tagging conventions that doesn't matter now but probably will in the future when the next iteration of HTML is out and about.

Recap II

So here's where we are. You've got the following tags down:

```
<HTML> </HTML>
<HEAD> </HEAD>
<!      >
<TITLE> </TITLE>
<BODY> </BODY>
<H1> </H1>
<H2> </H2>
<P> </P>
<BR>
<HR>
```

Figure 3.3 and Figure 3.4 show examples of what it all looks like so far.

Figure 3.3: *Using the Header <H1>, Paragraph <P>, Line Break <BR> and Rules <HR> tags (text).*

```
<HTML>

<HEAD>

<!--This is an example of the use of the Header, Paragraph,-->
<!--and Rules tags-->

<TITLE>American Diabetes Association</TITLE>

</HEAD>


<BODY>

<H1>Diabetes Texas WWW Server</H1>

Welcome to the Diabetes Texas WWW Home Page brought to you by the Texas Affiliate
of the Amercian Diabetes Association.<P>

The American Diabetes Association, Texas Affiliate is the leading diabetes-related
volunteer organization in Texas as well as the authoritative source of information
for the Texas diabetes commmunity - for people with diabetes, their families and
their health care providers.<P>

<H2>Current Research</H2>

<UL>
<LI><A HREF="ada/adaresearch/gennid.html">The GENNID Study</A<BR>
<LI><A HREF="ada/adaresearch/dcct.html">DCCT</A<BR>
<LI><A HREF="ada/adaresearch/type1trial.html">Type I Prevention Trial</A<BR>
<LI><A HREF="ada/adaresearch/adafunded.html">ADA Funded Research</A<BR>
<LI><A HREF="ada/adaresearch/volopps.html">Volunteer Opportunities</A<BR>
<LI><A HREF="ada/adaresearch/news.html">Addtional Research News</A<BR>
</UL>
<HR>


<ADDRESS>webmaster@dtx.org</ADDRESS>

</BODY>

</HTML>
```

Figure 3.4: *HTML code in Figure 3.3 viewed with a browser (Netscape).*

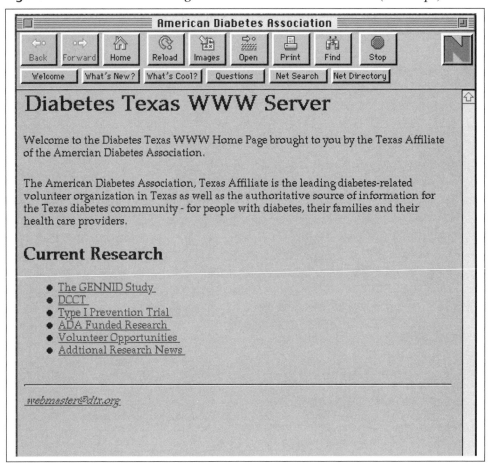

Logical Tags

If you want to play around with text attributes in a block of text and make it bold or italic, there are a couple of tags to use. Many WebMasters have been using the Bold <B> </B> and Italic <I> </I> tags as well as the Underline <U> </U> tag to accomplish this. Don't. If you have, consider changing your evil ways. This is one of those cases where we're going to teach you the right way to do it.

Italic, Bold, and Underline tags are referred to in the HTML world as "physical" styles. Physical styles are bad unless you have a good reason for using them. Instead, use what are referred to as "logical" styles and use the Strong **<STRONG> </STRONG>** tag for bold and the Emphasis **<EM> </EM>** tag for italics. Logical tags help enforce consistency in your documents and offer the browser the flexibility to display such tags with the user's preference.

In our humble opinion, you should never use the Underline **<U> </U>** tag. Just Don't Do It. Why? 'Cause the Underline command creates massive confusion, since most browsers display hypertext links with an underline.

Logical Markup Codes

Table 3.1 lists the logical markup types, their names and what they are used for, and how they typically appear.

Try these out on your own. Try them all. For the most part, you can just take the same text and use the different tags.

There's another physical style in addition to the Bold, Italic, and Underline we mentioned earlier. It's the infrequently seen Fixed Width **<TT> </TT>** tag. This tag gives a fixed-width typewriter text font. Like the other physical styles, we don't recommend it. Instead, use the logical tags **<CODE>** or **<SAMP>**.

Table 3.1: *Logical markup codes in HTML.*

Code	Used for	Typical appearance
<CITE> </CITE>	Citation; use for titles of books, films, etc.	Usually appears as italics when viewed in a browser.
<CODE> </CODE>	Code; use to show an example of computer code.	Usually appears as a fixed-width font when viewed in a browser.
<DFN> </DFN>	Defining instance; use for word being defined.	Usually appears as italics when viewed in a browser.
<EM> </EM>	Emphasis; use for emphasis.	Usually appears as italics when viewed in a browser.

Table 3.1:   *Logical markup codes in HTML. (continued)*

Code	Used for	Typical appearance
<KBD> </KBD>	Keyboard input; use for user keyboard entry.	Usually appears as bold or plain fixed-width font when viewed in a browser.
<SAMP> </SAMP>	Literal characters; use for computer status messages.	Usually displayed as a fixed-width font when viewed in a browser.
<STRIKE> </STRIKE>	Strike-out; use to show strike-out text. This tag is often used for legal documents.	Usually displayed as—you guessed it—text with a strike line through it when viewed in a browser.
<STRONG> </STRONG>	Strong emphasis; use for strong emphasis.	Usually appears as bold when viewed in a browser.

The PRE, BLOCKQUOTE, and ADDRESS Tags

Sometimes it is necessary to display text just as you want it to look, in a preformatted manner. You can do this with the Preformatted tag, <PRE> </PRE>. Other tags, attributes, and links can be used within the <PRE> tag. Figures 3.5 and 3.6 show an example.

You can also use the Block Quote command <BLOCKQUOTE> </BLOCKQUOTE> to display quoted text. Figures 3.7 and 3.8 give an example of that.

The ADDRESS Tag

There's one last tag that doesn't fall into any family — the Address tag, <ADDRESS> </ADDRESS>. Normally this is found at the end of page and holds contact information such as **webmaster@webmaster-win.com** (see Figures 3.7 and 3.8).

Figure 3.5: *Using the Preformatted tag <PRE> </PRE> (text).*

```
    <PRE>
                                    12 weeks ended

                                July 3        July 4
                                 1994          1993


    Sales                       $97,362       $79,518

    Cost of good sold and
      occupancy costs            65,871        53,773
    Direct expenses             23,716        19,075
    Pre-opening costs              384           416
    Amortization expense           261           194
    General and administrative
      expenses                   3,464         3,084
    Non-recurring expenses
      related to earthquake        --            --

        Income from operations   3,666         2,976

    </PRE>
```

Figure 3.6: *HTML code in Figure 3.5 viewed with a browser (Netscape).*

```
                            12 weeks ended

                        July 3        July 4
                         1994          1993


Sales                   $97,362       $79,518

Cost of good sold and
  occupancy costs        65,871        53,773
Direct expenses         23,716        19,075
Pre-opening costs          384           416
Amortization expense       261           194
General and administrative
  expenses               3,464         3,084
Non-recurring expenses
  related to earthquake    --            --

    Income from operations 3,666        2,976
```

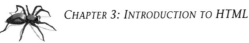

Figure 3.7: *Using the <BLOCKQUOTE> </BLOCKQUOTE> tag (text).*

```
<HTML>

<HEAD>

<!--This is an example of the BLOCKQUOTE Tag-->

<TITLE>American Diabetes Association</TITLE>

</HEAD>


<BODY>

<H1>Diabetes Texas WWW Server</H1>


Welcome to the Diabetes Texas WWW Home Page brought to you by the Texas
Affiliate of the Amercian Diabetes Association. The American Diabetes
Association, Texas Affiliate is the leading diabetes-related volunteer
organization in Texas as well as the authoritative source of information
for the Texas diabetes commmunity - for people with diabetes,
their families and their health care providers.<P>

<BLOCKQUOTE>The mission of the ADA is to prevent and cure diabetes and to
improve the lives of all people affected by diabetes.  Each year tens of
thousands of Texans are diagnosed with diabetes or find themselves facing
one of its many complications.<P></BLOCKQUOTE>

Our most innovative programs to date are the Diabetes Texas WWW Home Page
and our FirstClass based online service Diabetes Texas Online. Both are
timely and powerful ways to obtain reliable information and referrals as
well as access our extensive databases using the Texas Resource Directory.<P>


<HR>


<ADDRESS>webmaster@dtx.org</ADDRESS>

</BODY>

</HTML>
```

Entities and ISO Latin-1 Characters

There is a small set of character combinations referred to in HTML as entities, which are used to represent characters that have special meanings in HTML such as <, >, &, and ". There is also a large set of character combinations called the ISO Latin-1 characters that are used to represent

Figure 3.8: *HTML code in Figure 3.7 viewed with a browser (Netscape).*

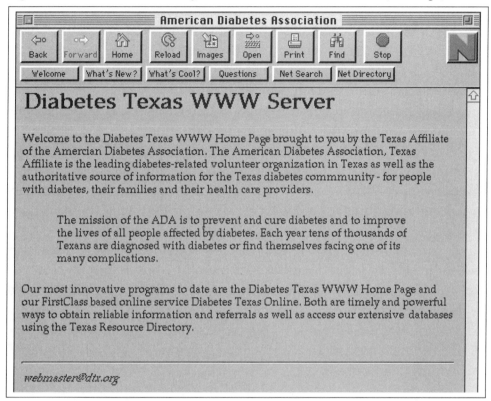

things like the n tilde (ñ), o slash (ø), and so on. The list of both — entities and Latin-1 characters — can be found in the appendices at the end of the book. By the way: Unlike the rest of HTML, entities and ISO Latin-1 characters are case-sensitive.

Lists, Lists, and Lists — How Many Ways Can You Make a List Already?
OK, we're getting close to the end of the tag stuff. Lists are next — a tag element you can get creative with. Kind of.

HTML supports three flavors of lists: unnumbered, numbered, and definition. You can also do lists within lists, which can be a very good thing.

Let's create two different types of lists, the unnumbered and numbered. The only difference between an unnumbered list and a numbered list is that the unnumbered list uses the Unnumbered List <UL> </UL> tag, whereas the numbered list uses the Ordered List <OL> </OL> tag. Items in the numbered list are then numbered; items in the unnumbered list are not. It's that simple.

The items listed in both instances begin with the List <LI> tag. Note that there is no need to include a closing </LI> tag.

You can use the Paragraph <P> tag or the Line Break <BR> tag — by inserting one or more, either, or both — to alter the spacing of the items in your list. You should know that by all accounts this is a completely bogus way of fooling around with HTML —but hey, what the heck, give it a try.

Figures 3.9 and 3.10 are examples of both types of legitimate lists and some playing around with nonstandard line breaks and spacing.

Another type of list is the definition list, which is sometimes called a "glossary." Definition lists consist of alternating a term and a definition. Within a definition list you can use all of the formatting tags except the heading tag and you can nest unnumbered and numbered lists within definition lists.

You use the <DL> </DL> tag to start and end a glossary, the <DT> tag for the main entry or subject line, and the <DD> tag for the descriptive text itself. The <DT> and <DD> tags have no end tags.

You got all that? Figures 3.11 and 3.12 show a great example.

The last two tags you need to know are the Anchor <A> </A> tag and the Image <IMG> tag. Both of these tags require that you define what you want them to do. That's what attributes are all about and we'll talk about them right after we look at…

You Are What You L: The Low-Down on URLs

We said that there were three parts to HTML: tags, attributes, and URLs. We're done with tags. Next we'll knock off URLs. We'll cover the slightly more complicated subject of attributes in a moment.

Figure 3.9: *Using the Unnumbered <UL> and Numbered List <OL> tags (text).*

```
<UL>
<LI>capers
<LI>olives
<LI>olive oil
<LI>red wine vinegar
<LI>pepper and salt
<LI>cayenne
<LI>italian seasoning
<LI>garlic and red onion
</UL>


<OL>
<LI>capers
<LI>olives
<LI>olive oil
<LI>red wine vinegar
<LI>pepper and salt
<LI>cayenne
<LI>italian seasoning
<LI>garlic and red onion
</OL>


<A HREF="http://www.gnn.com">GNN Home Page</A><BR>
<A HREF="http://www.iquest.net/cgi-bin/cr/">I-Quest</A><BR>
<A HREF="http://www.txinfinet.com">MahaInfinet WWW Server</A><BR><P>

<OL>
<A HREF="http://www.gnn.com">GNN Home Page</A><BR>
<A HREF="http://www.iquest.net/cgi-bin/cr/">I-Quest</A><BR>
<A HREF="http://www.txinfinet.com">MahaInfinet WWW Server</A><BR>
</OL>

<UL>
<A HREF="http://www.gnn.com">GNN Home Page</A><BR>
<A HREF="http://www.iquest.net/cgi-bin/cr/">I-Quest</A><BR>
<A HREF="http://www.txinfinet.com">MahaInfinet WWW Server</A><BR>
</UL>
```

You know by now that URL stands for Uniform Resource Locator. (It's not Uniform Resource Location or Uniform Record Locator. It's Uniform Resource Locator. We've heard and seen all these and worse.)

Figure 3.10: *HTML code in Figure 3.9 viewed with a browser (Netscape).*

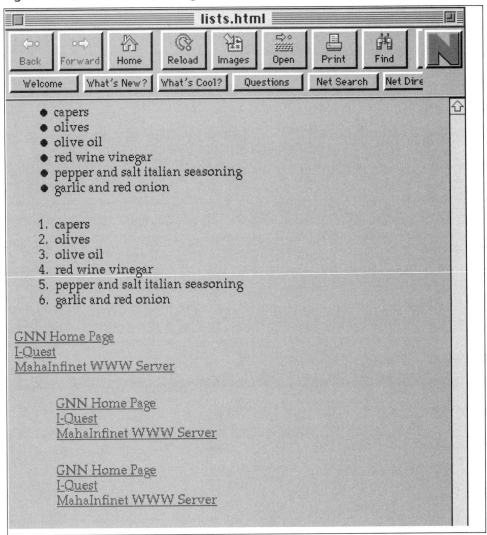

The Web uses URLs to find files on servers. If you want to place links to other sites or files on the Net in your Web pages, you need to know how to use URLs.

Figure 3.11: *The Definition List <DL>, </DL>, <DT>, and <DD> tags (text).*

```
<H2>Diabetes Texas WWW Services</H2>

<DL>
<DT>Diabetes Information and Action Line (D.I.A.L.) Manual
<DD>The D.I.A.L. Manual contains answers to your most frequently
asked questions about diabetes, as well as referrals to relevant
publications.<P>

<DT>Texas Resource Directory
<DD>The Texas Resource Directory is an easily searchable database
with over 6,000 sources of information and assistance for Texans
affected by diabetes.  These resources can be found using dozens of
categories organized into major topic groups as well as by city,
county and ADA Chapter.<P>

<DT>Diabetes Texas Online
<DD>Diabetes Texas Online is a FirstClass online service that offers a
graphical user interface for both Mac and Windows-based PC users over
dial up modem lines throughout Texas.<P>

<DT>Publications Center
<DD>A comprehensive listing of the publications available from the
American Diabetes Association, Texas Affiliate and others including a brief
summary of each together with ordering information.<P>

<DT>Scientific Research
<DD>Information about the latest scientific research studies on diabetes.<P>

<DT>Legislative Alerts
<DD>Legislative agendas that impact the Texas diabetes community as well
as a directory of Texas state legislators.<P>
</DL>
```

A URL "address" has the following defined format:

```
scheme://host.domain [:port]/path/filename
```

Yum. It's that UNIX stuff, back to haunt us. You need to understand it, though, if you're going to do links properly. And since links are what it's all about, take a deep breath and dive in.

Here's what that gobbledygook means.

The *scheme* can be one of the following:

- **file://** — a file on your local system or on an anonymous FTP server
- **http://** — a file on a WWW server
- **ftp://** — a file on an anonymous FTP server

Figure 3.12: *HTML code in Figure 3.11 viewed with a browser (Netscape).*

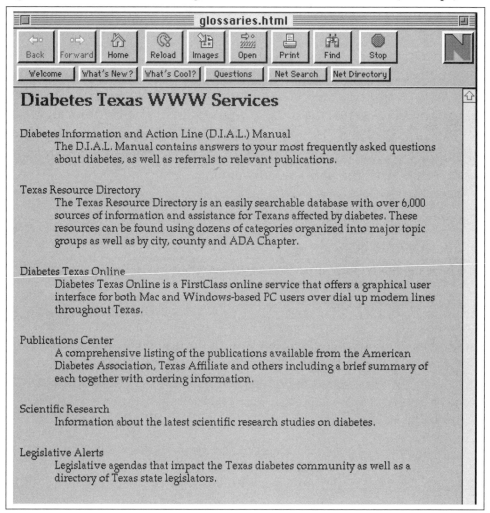

- **gopher://** — a file on a Gopher server
- **wais://** — a file on a WAIS server
- **news://** — UseNet newsgroup
- **telnet://** — a connection to a Telnet-based service

The *host.domain* part refers to the machine name (if any) and domain name of the server you want to link to.

The *[:port]* part of the URL syntax is usually not included when you create a link. (The default port for WWW servers is 80, by the way.) But it's part of the official spec, so we had to tell you about it. Unless you see it indicated in the URL of a place you want to link to, leave it out.

The *path/filename* is everything after the domain name (and port, if any). It shows what directories or folders you have to nest your way down through to get to the file you want to link to. Sometimes all you'll want to link to is the "Home Page" of a WWW server, or the top-level directory of an FTP site, for instance. In that case you don't have to concern yourself with the path and filename.

The Absolute Theory of HTML Relativity

There are two types of links that are often confusing to beginning HTMLers: the relative and the absolute links.

A relative URL is a URL that doesn't contain all the parts of an absolute URL — such as the type of scheme (**http://**, **ftp://**, **telnet://**, etc.) and host name and full path to the document. You can safely use relative links to documents when the linked document is in the same directory or when the document is on the same level as the server itself. A couple of examples of using relative URLs are:

```
<A HREF = "bestsites.html">My Hotlist</A>
```

and

```
<A HREF = "/futureplans.html">Plans for Future
Growth</A>
```

An absolute link would be more along the lines of:

```
<A HREF = "http://webmasterwin.com/bestsites.html>My
Hotlist</A>
```

Attributes

To create a link, you need to use the Anchor <A> </A> tag. Anchor tags are used when you want to link to another location or when you want to use hypertext links to navigate through large documents. The Anchor tag requires an attribute to tell it exactly what to do. There are two attributes for the Anchor tag: the HREF attribute and the NAME attribute. Let's take HREF first.

HREFs

The following format is used for an Anchor tag with an HREF attribute (the spaces before and after the equals signs aren't necessary):

```
<A HREF = "filename">HYPERTEXT</A>
```

For example:

```
<A HREF = "http://www.wholefoods.com/wf.html">Whole Foods</A>
```

Notice how the beginning of the Anchor tag isn't just <A>. The whole thing up to the "W" in "wholefoods" is the first part of the Anchor tag. Then comes the word or words that the user will see as a hypertext link with their browser (e.g., **Whole Foods**), followed by the rest of the Anchor tag, </A>. When the user clicks on the words **Whole Foods** on the screen, the browser will surf to **http://www.wholefoods.com/wf.html**. Neat, huh?

Just stare at it a couple of times if you didn't get that the first time through.

NAMEs

The other type of attribute to use with an Anchor tag is the NAME attribute. You use a NAME attribute and an HREF attribute together to make it easier and more interesting and fun to navigate through large text documents. The format for an anchor with NAME attribute is as follows:

```
<A NAME = "name">TEXT</A>
```

For example, say you have a long text filename "WF.food.html" (Document A) with a section we want to link to from another document (Document B). You use the NAME attribute as follows:

```
<A NAME = "cafedeli">

The Whole Foods Café and Deli satisfies the concerns of even the pickiest
eaters at a glance. Easy-to-read nutrition cards itemize calories, fat,
protein, carbohydrates, sodium, and cholesterol, and indicate food ex-
change equivalents. You get fresh food fast at the Whole Foods Deli. Wheth-
er you eat it on the run or in our Cafe, you'll enjoy fantastic flavors
and creative combinations of natural foods.</A>
```

In this example, you define the section of Document A, beginning with the words "The Whole Foods Cafe" as the place that will be linked to from another document.

On another document about Whole Foods (or any document for that matter) we create a link to the "NAMEd" part of Document A by using an anchor with the HREF attribute. Wherever we want a link to the section that has been "NAMEd", all we have to do is follow the format:

```
<A HREF = "linked file" NAME = "#name">Hypertext Anchor</A>
```

For example:

```
<A HREF = "WF.food.html"#cafedeli>Cafe and Deli</A>
```

If the link to a "NAMEd" section is within the same document (e.g., from one place in Document A to another place in Document A) it is not necessary to include the "linked file" part of the HREF attribute. In that case, do this:

```
<A HREF = #cafedeli>Cafe and Deli</A>
```

Don't forget to include the **#** mark before the text used to define the NAME! Oh yeah, we almost forgot. The text you use to define your NAME has to be a one-word name.

Whew!

If you got that first time around either your mind is a sponge or we are beyond awesome ... and less than humble. It's a bit tricky. Anchors with the NAME attribute are probably the hardest part of HTML to grok at first. Whenever we use them we always go back and read up on them quietly. There's no point memorizing this stuff when you have a book to help you, right?

Ultimately, practice makes perfect, so play around with anchors and attributes a bit before we continue with images.

Images <IMGs>

Graphics are a cool addition to your Web pages. We'll show you the things you can do with HTML to place your graphics on your page and even show you how to use a picture as a link.

Just for laughs, you should know that if your graphics stink we won't be able to help you. Neither one of us can draw to save our lives. Hopefully you, or someone you know, can create decent graphics.

It's not just a matter of taste by the way. Keep in mind that not everyone has an ISDN line to their house or office. Most people seeing your Web pages will be doing it via 14.4 or 28.8 modems. Put another way: If you have graphics that are huge it's OK if they are ugly, because no one is going to wait for them to load anyway.

Inline vs. External (Linked) Images

You can present graphics on your page as either inline or linked. Inline images are images that appear within the page, automatically. Linked images are images that stand alone and are linked to and reside elsewhere — either on the same server or elsewhere on the Internet. You have to click to see a linked image; an inline image appears automatically when a browser comes across it (assuming that preference is turned on in the user's browser). Inline images must be either in GIF or XBM format because that's all the image types that HTML currently supports.

In general, you want to use external images when the images are too large to be inline. We think that anything over 100K is way too big to be an inline image — unless your site is a big-time image site and you warn people in advance. If it's such a great image and you really need it in order to get your message across, make it an external image so that it doesn't slow down the loading of your text.

There are really only a couple of other reasons to link to an external image. An image may need to be linked as an external image if it resides on another server for reasons such as Web server performance optimization or storage location, or because the image is not a GIF or XBM image. Remember that when you link to other types of graphic images such as JPEG, you are dependent on the user having the helper app that will launch to show it. It's tough nugies for the user who doesn't have the helper apps and pity on those who use a browser — like Lynx — that doesn't display images at all.

Inserting Inline Images

You can insert an inline image by using the Image **<IMG>** tag. There's no end tag involved. It's just **<IMG>**. The **<IMG>** tag is another one of those tags that requires an attribute. In this case it's the **SRC** (source) attribute, which is used to define the filename of... the source! The **SRC** attribute can be any URL. The format for the **<IMG>** tag is:

```
<IMG SRC = image_URL>
```

For example:

```
<IMG SRC = sriyantra.gif>
```

Remember, you have to use the **.gif** or **.xbm** extension if the file is a GIF or XBM file and you want it to load as an inline image.

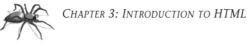

Inserting Linked Images

If you wanted to create a linked image, linking to a graphic stored on another server, it would look something like this:

```
<A HREF="http://www.txinfinet.com/gifs/sriyantra.gif">Wealth and
Prosperity</A>.
```

There are a couple of other attributes you can add to the <**IMG**> tag that define how text is displayed after an image. As HTML formally stands, you can use the **ALIGN** attribute and position text adjacent to an image using values of **TOP, MIDDLE,** or **BOTTOM.** The formats for doing this are as follows:

```
<IMG ALIGN = TOP SRC = bob.gif>My name is Bob LeVitus.
<IMG ALIGN = MIDDLE SRC = jeff.gif>My name is Bob LeVitus.
<IMG ALIGN = BOTTOM SRC = carl.gif> My name is Bob LeVitus.
```

Figure 3.13 shows the HTML and Figure 3.14 shows how those three examples turn out on the screen.

Figure 3.13: *Will the Real Bob LeVitus Please Stand Up (text).*

```
<H2>Will the Real Bob Levitus Please Stand Up</H2>

<A HREF="bobsbio.html"><IMG SRC="bob.gif" ALIGN=TOP></A>My name is Bob Levitus<P>
<A HREF="bobsbio.html"><IMG SRC="bob.gif" ALIGN=MIDDLE></A>My name is Bob Levitus<P>
<A HREF="bobsbio.html"><IMG SRC="bob.gif" ALIGN=BOTTOM></A>My name is Bob Levitus<P>
```

If for some sick reason you feel you need to do something for the Lynx users out there (Lynx is a semi-ancient text-only browser rarely used these days), you can use the ALT attribute to show some text as an alternative to the image. You can let them see the words "meow" instead of a picture of Socks, the White House cat and most frequented part of the WWW server at the White House (**http://www.whitehouse.gov**)

Figure 3.14: *HTML code in Figure 3.13 viewed with a browser (Netscape).*

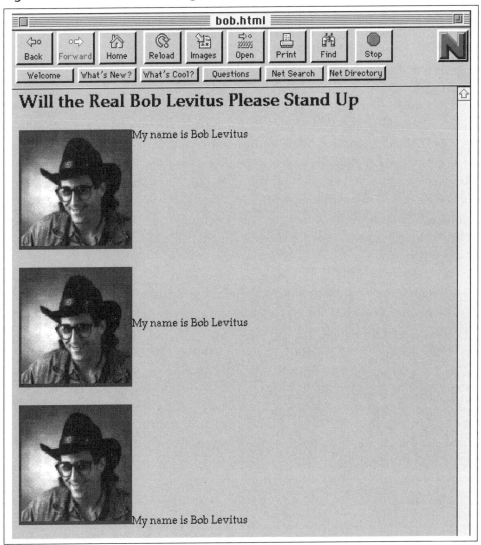

The format for the ALT attribute that goes with the IMG tag is:

```
<IMG SRC = "cat.gif" ALT = "meow">
```

Finally, there are plenty of tricks in the following sidebar, which was written for us by one of our favorite WebMistresses, Julie Gomoll.

Designing for the Web

by Julie Gomoll, President, Go Media, Inc.

Your computer screen is not a piece of paper. Most printed material is presented in a fashion that reflects decades of graphic design knowledge. We know what point size and leading make for the most readable novel, and we know that the brain assimilates information differently when it encounters sans serif type on glossy white paper than it does bright red type on neon yellow paper. Photographers know that part of the impact of a picture assumes the viewer will be seeing it at a certain size, from a specific distance, under controlled lighting. Information in a brochure is designed with the confidence that the reader will approach the material in a linear fashion, starting *here* and ending there.

Needless to say, the Web is another story. People are designing Web pages as though the screen were just another print medium. Online magazines are laid out like newsrack publications. Electronic catalogs appear to be direct adaptations of their printed counterparts.

Think about the information you're designing. The amount of information you can present in a square inch of screen real estate is practically nothing compared to the amount you can put in the same amount of paper space. You're limited in the fonts you can use, and you can't assume everyone will be looking at your site using the same-quality monitor you've been using. Your audience may not even be bothering to load your graphics. You can count on the fact that if you're using more than a couple of hypertext links, users at the other end will be meandering through your masterpiece in a manner that makes sense to *them*. So — a few tips:

- Keep your home page simple. Give the viewer a chance to choose the area at your site that is most interesting. Don't assume they'll be willing to scroll through several feet of screen in hopes of finding something interesting.

- If you use a clickable map, offer a text version of the same links for the poor souls trying to surf with their trusty old 9600 baud modems.

Designing for the Web (continued)

- Put the size of the graphic in parentheses near the icon, so users know what they're in for if they decide to look at it.

- Offer a return route. Dead-end pages can be a pain, and some folks bounce around in such a way that the "back" button in their browser isn't a very efficient option.

- Keep your graphics small. *(More on that in a moment ...)*

A Couple of More Fun Things Before We Leave

There are a couple of fun things you can do with anchors, graphics and external links that we'd like to touch on before turning you loose to try some of this out on your own.

You can make a graphic an anchor for a hypertext link. You already know all the pieces of HTML markup that we used to do this. But if you're like us, it's easier if we just show it to you. Here it is:

```
<A HREF = "CyberSurfing.html"><IMG SRC="ganesh.gif"</A>
```

If I click on the image of Lord Ganesh, it takes me to the document called CyberSurfing.html. You can see an example of this function on the examples page of the WebMaster Windows WWW server.

The other cool thing you can do now that you know the syntax for external images is to create links on your documents to other types of externals. The only difference is the file type of the linked file. Here's an example:

```
<A HREF = "MyFavoriteSound.au>Listen to this!</A>
```

Carl pointed out that this is also an example of bad form. It's almost as bad as **Click here!** Say what the sound is. At least be a little more creative than **Listen to this!**

You can link to all sorts of things — audio, movies, graphics, or sounds (as shown above). You can have loads of fun with linked files. Try some of these:

Table 3.2: *Linked file types and their extensions.*

File type	Extension
Plain text	.txt
HTML document	.htm
GIF image	.gif
TIFF image	.tif
XBM bitmap image	.xbm
JPEG image	.jpg
PostScript file	.ps
AIFF sound	.aif
AU sound	.au
QuickTime movie	.mov
MPEG movie	.mpg

Just remember: As we mentioned earlier, not everyone will have the proper external apps — such as a JPEG viewer or sound player — to enjoy these multimedia links. But hey, we say push the envelope and leave it up to them to get the helper apps they need. (If you want to be a really cool WebMaster, give them a link to an FTP site that has your favorites.)

HTML: Top 10 Tips and Avoiding Common Errors

There are all sorts of pitfalls to avoid when you're doing HTML. Some of them are technical, others are aesthetic. We're going to zero in on the technical ones — the ones where you screw up and write some HTML that either doesn't come out right when you look at it with your browser, or is impossible to decipher when you go back to look at it months from now.

It's kind of a rule with HTML. Everyone gets nailed eventually. You will too. But rest assured, the more you play with HTML the less frequently it'll happen to you.

In a blatant attempt to save you at least a bit of time and trouble, here's our Top 10 list of tips and things to avoid:

10. Avoid improper use of the <P> tag to force a line break and carriage return.

Don't use the <P> tag before or after tags that carry their own line break such as <HR>, <PRE>, <ADDRESS>, <BLOCKQUOTE>, <UL>, <OL> and the Header tags <H1 ... H6>. You'll end up with extra white space on your page.

9. Be consistent with your styles.

Use uppercase with your HTML tags. Even though you still can get away with mixing cases and be all over the upper, lower, middle case map —use uppercase. Be consistent. Add some space in your HTML code when you use a <P> or a <HR>. (Browsers ignore white space!) And try to keep list items on single lines in your HTML code. Habits like these make it easier to read your HTML and you'll be less likely to forget the ending tags if your code is easy to read.

8. Don't forget the trailing semicolon after entities and ISO Latin-1 characters.

Remember — if you need to use the **&** entity to display the & (ampersand) to a browser, don't forget the semicolon that goes after the letters **amp**. It's

&

not

```
&amp
```

This rule also applies to ASCII or other character combinations used to represent the Latin-1 characters.

7. Use fully qualified domain names in URLs.

When you use a URL in a link be sure to use the entire fully qualified domain name (or IP number if that is all there is). Not everyone in the world is on the local network your Web server is on. You can't just give the link to the machine followed by the path to the document. For instance, if you were to use the link:

```
<A HREF="http://www/~sonya/graphics">Sonya's Graphics</A>
```

only the in-house troops on your local-area network will be able to see Sonya's awesome design work. You need to use the whole domain name to let the world in:

```
<A HREF="http://www.gomedia.com/~sonya/graphics">
Sonya's Graphics</A>
```

6. Avoid improper use of relative and absolute links.

In general, it is a good idea to use relative links — if you know what you are doing. They save typing because they're shorter. They also make it easier to move groups of HTML documents to another server since the path names to the documents are … relative, so you don't have to type in a new domain name for every linked document you are serving up.

The rule in a nutshell is to use absolute links when you are linking to other sites or sets of documents that are not grouped logically together.

5. Avoid improper use of the trailing / slash on URLs.

Here's one that no one seems to know much about outside the orbit of the HTML gods. Sometimes you'll see a trailing / slash at the end of a URL. Do you know what that's for? It's used to get the HTTP server to return an index of a directory. The server's response will be to either generate HTML on the fly and return a list of all the files in the directory to which you're linking or to return the contents of a file named index.html.

Bet you didn't know that. We sure didn't.

If you really do want the index.html or you want the server and directory to which you're linked to return the contents of the directory on the fly, use the / at the end of the URL. Otherwise don't. In other words, use:

```
http://www.gomedia.com/graphics
```

and not

```
http://www.goemedia.com/graphics/
```

Though most servers will redirect you to the proper URL, not all browsers support such transparent redirection. Once again, we suggest you do it right in the first place.

4. Use headings properly.

Be sure to use only heading levels that are one level below the level above. In other words, go from <H1> to <H2>. Don't follow an H1 heading with an H3 unless that's part of your design. In general, don't skip a level if you are using multiple heading elements. Besides being bad style, it is strictly verboten by Herr Shultz and HTML specification.

3. Avoid missing quotes in URL links.

Here's Jeff's biggie: Don't forget both the start and end quotes in your URL links — before and after! It's:

```
<A HREF="http://www.gomedia.com">
```

not

```
<A HREF="http://www.gomedia.com>
```

or

```
<A HREF=http://www.gomedia.com">
```

Look carefully until you see the difference. Only the first example will work. Try it for yourself and see what happens.

2. **Don't forget end tags.**

   Here's Jeff's other biggie: Don't forget the end tags. Actually, Jeff doesn't usually forget the end tag. He forgets the / in the end tag. Right:

```
<H1>My Favorite Web Sites</H1>
```

Wrong:

```
<H1>My Favorite Web Sites<H1>
```

You usually won't goof on one like this one. It's the ones where you have a long list of URL links that catch you. That's usually where you'll forget to use a / to close the tag. Those are also the links in which you forget the quotes in the URL link address — especially when you have a big old list of 'em.

We guess the moral of the story is to test your links thoroughly before unleashing your pages on the World (Wide Web).

And our number one tip?

1. **Buy HoTMetaL Pro so you don't have to type so much HTML! Or at least check out the demo version.**

   'Nuff said. It's wonderful.

One More Thing (Fixing Anchors) ...

We didn't want to upset the symmetry of our Top 10 list but we do have one last piece of advice for you. Whenever you are doing an anchor, be sure you open and close the quotes of the HREF attribute, be sure you have all the less than (<) and greater than (>) symbols for the anchor tags, and be sure you have the forward slash (/) before the closing anchor tag. Nine times out of ten, one of those points will be the reason your HTML doesn't look right when viewed with your browser.

Parting Shots

You can go off on all sorts of esoteric tangents talking about HTML. If you really want to tap into the HTML scene go visit the HAL Computer Systems HTML validation server at **http://www.hal.com/users/connolly/ html-test/service/about.html.** You can submit your HTML to their server and automatically get back a response telling you whether or not you've done it right. If you pass you are an absolute ace, an HTML guru.

The other thing you can do if you want to go deep in to the transcendent with HTML is read an HTML book, such as *HTML Programming For Dummies* by Ed Tittel (IDG Books).

You don't have to memorize everything in this chapter but you have to know how to do it to be a Master. You know where to turn if you forget. Feel free to take a highlighter to this section of the book if it helps (hey, you paid for it already). It reminds us of the old joke:

Q. How do you get to Carnegie Hall?
A. Practice, practice, practice.

Today, it's more like:

Q: How do you become a Master-Blaster Ultra WebMaster?
A: Practice, practice, practice.

The point we're making is that it's a lot easier to do than it is to read about. For best results, if you haven't already, try each of the examples in this chapter. We deliberately kept the examples short to encourage you to experiment with your own stuff, not just type in our boring example text.

Just take a byte at a time (groan) and learn to enjoy it. But learn to enjoy it soon, because we'll be delving much deeper into HTML when we tackle forms and CGI. So before you move on, be sure to crank out some HTML.

At the very least, we'd like to see you get a simple home page together so you can use it in the next chapter. It will be much more fun (and far more productive) if you're working on your own stuff when we show you how to configure and optimize a Web server.

Chapter 4

MAXIMIZING YOUR WEBSERVER

Bells, Whistles and Screaming Daemons

There are several ways you can set WebServer's parameters before starting normal operations to tweak performance and features. Rather than reinventing the wheel, the nice people at Quarterdeck kindly gave us permission to lift their instruction manual for our purposes here.

Certain events may occur over the course of normal operations which may require configuration changes. For example, HTML documents may be moved to other directories, or server resources may be moved to other machines (or even to other servers). Quarterdeck WebServer comes complete with its own setup utility which makes changing these configuration options extremely simple (and is much easier than editing the configuration files manually).

To run the setup program, open the Quarterdeck WebServer program group and double-click on the WebServer Setup icon.

Here's a brief overview of WebServer configuration options. For more details on any of these features, please see the setup utility's online help.

- Administration and Logging: You can easily reconfigure installation options such as the server administrator's e-mail address, or location of the log files that keep track of all network transactions.

- Network Setup: These options include technical network information such as port number and timeout interval.

- Directory Listings: Quarterdeck WebServer can create directory listings that enable remote users to download files just by clicking on their file-names. This feature enables you to provide downloadable files without requiring remote users to use FTP. Depending on the configuration options you select, these directory listings can also contain clickable icons or display HTML "footnote" files automatically at the bottom of the listing. You can also configure the name of your server's home page.

- Aliasing and Redirection: Your HTML documents will contain links to other files on your server; other users may also have their own HTML documents which point to your server's files. If you relocate your HTML files to another directory, or to another server entirely, all those links become invalid. For this contingency, Quarterdeck WebServer has two features which will keep HTML links working even if the documents themselves are relocated: aliases and redirection. *Aliases* translate requests for one directory (the old directory name in existing links) to another directory on the same server (the new directory where the files are now located). *Redirection* is a very useful feature when you relocate your documents to another server; WebServer will "redirect" network requests to the new location automatically.

- MIME Types and Encoding: MIME types give the browser and server a means to cooperate when exchanging data: both the browser and the server agree on the "type" of data (HTML file, GIF graphic image format, and so on) and both behave accordingly. You can define your own MIME types and encodings to handle whatever special applications your server may need to support.

- Access Permissions: Your server may contain information not intended for public release, which you want to restrict to members of your company or to only certain authorized users. Quarterdeck WebServer supports two methods of access restriction: by host name or IP address, and by username/password authentication. Host name restriction allows only those users who have particular network addresses to access a certain area of the server (for example, only those users at "mycompany.com"). Username/password authentication requires that a user supply a username and password before his browser will display a restricted HTML document.

- User Management: Before you can impose user-level access restrictions, you need to define the usernames and passwords which Quarterdeck WebServer will apply to your restricted documents. WebServer provides a simple way to add, modify or delete users quickly and easily. You can also simplify document management by creating groups of users and granting (or denying) access to the entire group at once.

- Script Management: Web servers quite commonly run "scripts"—application programs which use browser-supplied data. Quarterdeck WebServer comes configured with appropriate directories for your custom script applications, and you can change this configuration if you want to execute scripts in different directories.

Server Resources: Forms, Scripts and CGI

The browser/server relationship does not begin and end with "home pages," HTML, and multimedia files. Using special HTML documents called *forms*, a user can enter and send information to custom-written application programs on a server.

Here are some examples of forms currently in use at various locations on the Internet:

- An Internet service provider uses forms for non-urgent technical service problems. Users fill out forms with fields for their eMail address and problem. When the browser submits the form to the server, the server forwards the information via eMail to the appropriate support personnel.

- A major studio uses a form to ask for viewer feedback on its recent blockbuster sequel. Questions include "Which of the sequels did you like best?" When the browser submits the form, the server sends the data to a program that tabulates the responses, and mails back to the user a special graphic as a "thank you" for filling out the survey.

- A university uses forms as a "front end" for a program that queries a database. Users submit a search string; the server sends the string to the search engine, which returns the requested information to the user wanted. Some of the WebServer test applications use HTML forms. You can use your browser's "document source" function if you want to look at the HTML commands used to create the form.

Scripts and CGI

Browsers use forms to submit information to server *scripts*. A script is essentially a program, but it does not need to be written in a compiled programming language. Some scripts are DOS "batch files" (sometimes called "shell scripts"), or use batch files to pass data to other programs. Other scripts use Windows' Visual Basic or other Windows-based programming languages. Non-DOS computers write scripts in a wide range of different script "languages." Exactly how you write a script depends on what you want that script to accomplish, so it is difficult in a guide such as this to give you a bird's-eye view of "what to put in a script." However, you can use the scripts included with WebServer's test documents to give you some idea of typical script functions and how to accomplish them.

One of the most important concepts to understand regarding scripts is exactly how the server communicates with scripts. Servers and scripts use something called CGI (Common Gateway Interface) to talk to one another. CGI itself is not a programming language; rather, it defines the interface, the method of interaction, that allows WebServer to execute and exchange information with scripts. There are separate CGI interfaces for DOS- and Windows-based scripts. In the DOS CGI interface, environment variables are used to pass information between the server and script. Because Windows does not support environment variables, a special interface was defined for Windows scripts. The Windows CGI interface uses data files, in Windows INI file format, to pass information between the server and script.

Which should you use, DOS-based or Windows-based scripts? Again, it depends on the nature of the application. Take a look at the different kinds of scripts included with WebServer's test documents for an idea of the different approaches DOS and Windows script applications take. DOS scripts provide an easy way to learn how CGI works. However, Windows scripts are much more efficient, and can run several times faster than DOS-based scripts. The heavier the use on your server, the more important it is for your scripts to run quickly and efficiently.

Some DOS CGI programmers prefer to use other command processors (that is, other than COMMAND.COM, the DOS command processor). Other command processors have more powerful and flexible methods of handling environment variables and command-line arguments. If you want an alternative command processor, you can configure script parameters to work with them. For more information, see the online help under Advanced Script Processor Options.

You can also get a great deal of information on CGI and scripting on the Internet. Some recommended addresses are contained in the online help: Search for the topic CGI technical overview.

A Final Note on Scripts

CGI is the most technical aspect of server management, and it requires programming ability to make full use of its possibilities. Most of the other server functions — log management, initial configuration, access controls, and even creating HTML documents — can be done by anyone with a background in computer operations and a little help from on- and off-line manuals. Working with scripts can be very technical. If you are not a programmer yourself, or if you have difficulty working with CGI and scripts, you may find it helpful to contact someone with programming experience for assistance with CGI or scripts.

Server Security

Whenever you are in charge of any aspect of computer operations that involves networks, you need to be aware of security concerns. Quarterdeck WebServer is not designed to be a "secure server," a term reserved for systems specially constructed both to handle confidential information and to be particularly robust against all manner of insidious attacks. Unless you are the administrator for your local network or an Internet service provider in your own right, most of the network's security worries will not be your concern (you may have already received at least one lecture on security from your network manager or service provider when you first asked about setting up WebServer). However, WebServer does have document access controls you can use to prevent unauthorized access to server files.

Quarterdeck WebServer's main line of defense against unauthorized access is its *virtual directory* structure based around the *document root directory.* When you set up WebServer, you designate one directory as the document root directory: the directory under which all HTML documents will be stored. WebServer then treats that directory as the "root directory" when it communicates with browsers.

Here is how it works. The table below shows how WebServer would convert the browser's request for files under a *virtual* root directory (which only exists for the browser) into the physical path by adding the name of the document root directory. In the example below (and by default), the document root directory is C:\HTTPD\HTDOCS.

The browser requests...	The server translates that into...
/PRODUCTS.HTM	C:\HTTPD\HTDOCS\PRODUCTS.HTM
/PICS/MAP.GIF	C:\HTTPD\HTDOCS\PICS\MAP.GIF

How does this enhance document security? Two ways. First, this masks the true directory structure of your server computer (and network security experts agree that the less information available about your server, the better). More importantly, the document root directory is completely separate from the server configuration files, including the password files; this means that no one can use normal server functions to view files crucial to your security setup.

Unless you are working in a completely secure and trusted environment, never make the document root directory the server's actual root directory. "Trusted" is an important security concept; it means that you trust absolutely everyone in the environment to have the same respect for the server that you do. If you make the document root directory the server's root directory, you will lose all the benefit and protection the document root directory affords you and create possible security breaches—and in the computer security world, a "possible" breach must be treated as a "probable," or even "certain," breach.

There is a second, non-security-related benefit to the virtual directory structure. If you store all of your HTML files in the same directory tree, you can use relative URLs in all your hypertext links between files. That is, you can omit absolute directory names, and just use relative paths in the links. If you ever need to move your document tree to another disk or another root directory, you can just change the document root directory, and make no changes to any of the HTML files — the links will all continue to work. See an HTML reference for more information on specifying URLs in hypertext links.

WebServer's second line of defense is called host filtering. A *host filter* allows or denies certain hosts (that is, network sites with unique host names or IP addresses) access to your server. For example, if you had confidential company information on your server, you would want to make sure that only users in "yourcompany.com" could use your server.

WebServer also has a third line of defense: *user authentication*. You can configure WebServer to demand a username and password from anyone wishing to access a particular directory. Or, to restrict access to the entire server, you can require a password before *any* document can be displayed by applying a password restriction to the document root directory.

Depending on your access control needs, you can combine host filtering and user authentication to create a flexible and sturdy document access system.

On the Internet, you can find many discussions of server security. Most of these regard concerns specific to servers on UNIX systems. You can disregard warnings regarding "rsh," "rlogin," "root," "suid" or problems with commands or file systems that clearly are not DOS-based. However, you may find interesting suggestions at the periphery of these discussions which are well worth your consideration.

- Whenever you make configuration changes using the WebServer setup utility, you have to shut down and restart the server to implement your changes.

Using CGI

CGI, which stands for Common Gateway Interface, is a way for Web clients (like Mosaic) and servers (like Quarterdeck WebServer) to exchange information with programs and databases. A CGI program can get information from the client and server, and it can send information—usually in the form of a new page, created on the fly—back to the client. You can create an HTML form which a user can fill out with a browser. Then, with CGI, you can retrieve the user's input and run a program on the server to process the information the user provided.

You can also use CGI to process imagemaps, which are images that have multiple "hot spots," regions of the image which contain invisible hypertext links. In an imagemap, clicking on a hot spot activates a link, leading the browser to its corresponding URL.

How Does a Client Run a CGI Application?
This is a very simple procedure. The author of an HTML file places the name of the program as the attribute to an anchor tag in his HTML document:

```
<A HREF="cgi-win/program.exe">Click here to run my script.</A>
```

When a user clicks on the link text, the browser sends a request to the server to execute the associated program.

How Does CGI Work?

CGI typically involves a server running a program that gets information from the client, processes information, and sends information to the client.

CGI programs can be written in any programming language, but in practice, each operating system has preferred languages. The language you use depends not only on the operating system you have, but on the interface you want to use. Here is a quick list:

- Windows servers: DOS command shell ("batch"), Visual Basic, C/C++
- UNIX servers: shell, Perl
- Macintosh servers: AppleScript, Frontier, MacPERL, HyperCard and C/C++

For Windows servers, like WebServer, the most popular languages are DOS command shell, Visual Basic, and C. Although Visual Basic and C are more powerful than DOS batch language in most ways, batch language is still a good starting place for learning about CGI, for two reasons:

- Batch programs are fairly straightforward, and require no compiling or interpreting before they are ready to test.
- DOS batch language strongly resembles UNIX shell scripts, which is the language you will find in most of the official CGI documentation available on the Internet. (Although DOS-based servers like Quarterdeck WebServer are becoming more popular, most of the Web servers in operation today use UNIX. If you know how to write DOS batch files using CGI, you will be able to understand most of the UNIX documentation.

Although batch files are an easy way to learn CGI, they do not execute as efficiently as Windows-based applications. When Windows executes a DOS application, it starts a "DOS virtual machine" that takes time and resources to maintain. To make the most efficient use of your server's computing resources—and to ensure the best response time—we recommend that you use Windows-based scripts whenever possible.

CGI and Data Exchange

There are several ways that data can flow between the client, server, and your CGI program:

- The client can send information to the server.
- The server can send information to your CGI program.
- Your CGI program can send information to the client via the server.

DOS- and Windows-based scripts handle data exchange differently. The next section describes how DOS scripts use CGI to exchange data (Windows CGI will be discussed later).

Sending Information from the Client to the Server

The client usually passes information to the server via two types of command-line options that have different forms: *query string* and *extra path*.

In a query string, data is passed by separating the data from the CGI program name with a question mark (?). For example:

```
<A HREF="cgi-win/program.exe?parameters">
```

Using the extra path method, data is passed by separating the data from the CGI program name with slashes (/). For example,

```
<A HREF="cgi-win/program.exe/parameter1/parameter2/parameter3">
```

Sending Information to Your CGI Program

The server takes query strings and extra path information and sends them to your CGI program in the environment variables QUERY_STRING and EXTRA_PATH. In addition, there are several other useful environment variables the server sets before calling your program. We will look briefly at these variables later.

Sending Information to the Client

WebServer scripts write their output to a special filename the server provides in the environment variable OUTPUT_FILE.

Sending Data to the Client—HELLO.BAT

The easiest way to get a feel for CGI is to look at some simple CGI programs. A good program to start with is one that creates some text and sends it to the client. This program will create a simple browser page that just says. "Hello, World Wide Web." [*] Here is HELLO.BAT:

```
echo Content-type: text/plain >%output_file%
echo. >>%output_file%
echo Hello, World Wide Web >>%output_file%
```

After the initial comment lines, you'll find the first, and in many ways most important, line in the program:

```
echo Content-type: text/plain >%output_file%
```

There are two important things about the mechanics of transferring information we see from this line:

- The program sends information to the server by writing to a file whose name is held in the environment variable OUTPUT_FILE. (In batch files, environment variables begin and end with percent signs.)
- The program writes text to this file using the DOS ECHO command and redirects its output to OUTPUT_FILE using the ">" symbol.

This is the basic technique used in all the DOS CGI programs: Use DOS batch commands (primarily ECHO) and redirect output to the variable %OUTPUT_FILE%.

Now, we will look at exactly what the program sends:

---

[*] These CGI scripts are provided courtesy of Velocity Research, who designed these
   scripts exclusively for Quarterdeck WebServer.

```
Content-type: text/plain
```

The Content-type header is the essential first line of all CGI-generated Web pages. It tells the browser what type of information follows. This particular line tells the browser that the following data is plain text. (The content type uses the MIME—Multipurpose Internet Mail Extensions—format to let the browser know what kind of data follows.)

The Content-type header must be followed by a blank line. In DOS batch language, we create a blank line with this interesting-looking code:

```
echo. >>%output_file%
```

The dot (.) echoes a blank line, which is redirected to %OUTPUT_FILE%. If you forget this blank line, your CGI program will fail, so be sure to put it in. Also, be sure to note that the first time we send output to %OUTPUT_FILE%, we use the redirection symbol (>). All subsequent redirections must *append* information to the file using the append symbol >>.

Once we have sent information to the browser telling it what kind of data is going to follow (the "Content-type" header plus its blank line), we can specify the data itself—the text the server is to send to the client:

```
echo Hello, World Wide Web >>%output_file%
```

This line echoes the words "Hello, World Wide Web" and redirects the output to OUTPUT_FILE.

Putting CGI Programs to Work

Now that we have finished the code, where do we put this program so we can run it, and how do we put a reference on a Web page to run it?

CGI programs go in a special directory or directories that are reserved for scripts. Quarterdeck WebServer has two directories: one for DOS programs and one for Windows programs. By default, these directories are:

- HTTPD\CGI-BIN\DOS for DOS programs
- HTTPD\CGI-BIN\WIN for Windows programs

To make referring to these directories easier, Quarterdeck WebServer uses two predefined script aliases:

- CGI-DOS is the alias for the DOS programs
- CGI-WIN is the alias for Windows programs

To run this program from an HTML page, you simply make it the target of a hypertext link using the HTML "anchor" command:

```
<A HREF="cgi-dos/hello.bat">Click here to run HELLO.BAT</A>
```

Because of the predefined script alias, the server knows that CGI-DOS holds executable programs, so it will not send HELLO.BAT to the client as a document; instead, the server will run HELLO.BAT as a program. HELLO.BAT in turn uses OUTPUT_FILE, the special environment variable the server has set up for it, to send data back to the client.

As you have gathered, this program prints "Hello, World Wide Web" on a new Web page (Figure 4.1).

HELLO.BAT is simple, but it demonstrates several key things about DOS CGI programs.

- The server sends data to the client using a special environment variable called %OUTPUT_FILE%.
- In a batch file, you preface each script command with an ECHO command, and redirect the output to %OUTPUT_FILE% using ">>" (or > for the first line only).
- The first line of any Web page created by a CGI program *must* be a "Content-type" header.
- The Content-type header *must* be followed by a blank line, produced by "ECHO." (ECHO followed immediately by a period—no spaces.)
- CGI programs go in a special directory (which Quarterdeck WebServer defines using a *script alias*).

Figure 4.1: *The output of HELLO.BAT.*

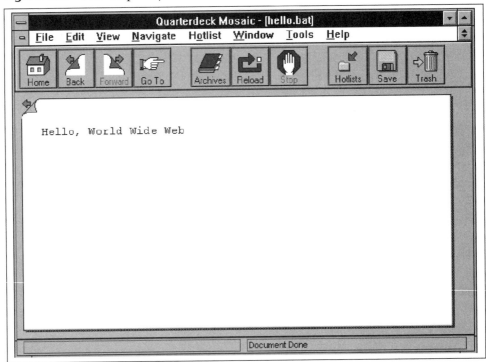

- When a client requests a program in a designated CGI directory, the server knows it is a CGI program and treats it accordingly.

Passing Parameters to a CGI Program

The most direct way to pass parameters to a CGI is to use a *query string*. To use a query string in the hypertext link, you simply separate the program's name and the parameter with a question mark:

```
<A HREF="cgi-dos/show.bat?hello.bat">Click here to run SHOW.BAT</A>
```

This line runs the program SHOW.BAT and passes HELLO.BAT to it as a query string parameter.

SHOW.BAT displays the file whose filename is passed to it as a query string. Here is the program:

```
echo Content-type: text/plain >%output_file%
echo. >>%output_file%
echo Text of %query_string% follows: >>%output_file%
echo. >>%output_file%
type %query_string% >>%output_file%
```

Notice again that the first line is the Content-type header and that it is followed by a blank line. The next two lines are a heading, and the final line returns the query string in the environment variable %query_string%:

```
type %query_string% >>%output_file%
```

Figure 4.2 illustrates what happens when we run the script.

Figure 4.2: *The output of SHOW.BAT.*

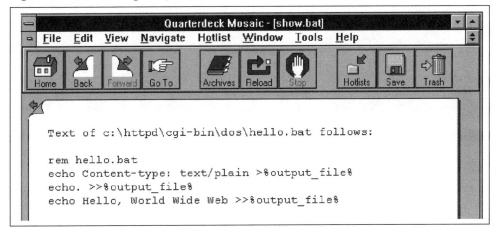

Environment Variables

As discussed earlier, environment variables are the principal way that information is passed to a DOS script from the server. There are a number of these variables, and it is surprisingly easy to get a picture of what they are and the information each holds. SET.BAT displays all the environment variables currently set on your system:

```
echo Content-type:text/plain > %output_file%
echo. >> %output_file%
echo DOS Environment Variables: >>%output_file%
echo. >> %output_file%
set >> %output_file%
echo. >> %output_file%
```

The initial lines echo the Content-type header

```
echo Content-type:text/plain > %output_file%
```

and display a heading

```
echo DOS Environment Variables: >>%output_file%
```

The key line issues the DOS SET command, which displays all the current environment variables, and redirects the output to %OUTPUT_FILE% (Figure 4.3).

```
set >> %output_file%
```

Figure 4.3: *The output of SET.BAT.*

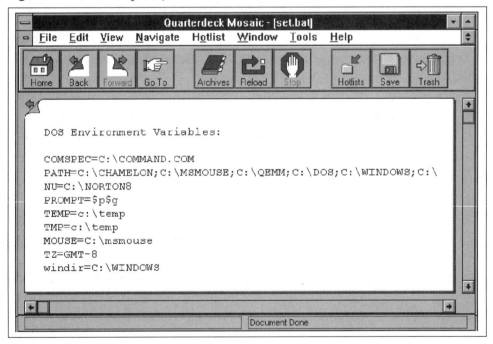

Formatting with DOS Programs

You have probably noticed that none of the DOS examples we have looked at so far uses HTML formatting. Everything has been sent as plain text (with the Content-type header "text/plain") rather than as HTML (with a Content-type of "text/html"). The reason for this is simple: HTML tags (the commands that do all the formatting) are placed inside angle brackets (<>). In DOS, these angle brackets are interpreted as redirection symbols, and as a consequence, there is no way to redirect an angle bracket because DOS thinks it is a command.

For example, to send a heading tag to our OUTPUT_FILE variable, you might try to do something like this:

```
echo <H1>This is a level one heading</H1> >>%output_file%
```

but this will *not* work. DOS would interpret "h1" as the name of a program whose output you are redirecting to the ECHO command.

You can get around this limitation, however, by putting chunks of HTML inside files, and using the TYPE command to redirect the contents of these files to %OUTPUT_FILE%.

The next example, SEARCH.BAT, does just that. It puts heading HTML text in two files called DIR1.TXT and DIR2.TXT and closing HTML data in a file called DIR3.TXT.

SEARCH.BAT also shows another interesting CGI technique, which is called ISINDEX searching. SEARCH.BAT searches the Web server for any file or files the user types into a search box. The program follows the pattern of all ISINDEX searches: The first time it is run, it tells the browser to display a box into which the user can type a search string (Figure 4.4). Pressing **Enter** causes the program to run again, but this time the browser passes the parameter the user typed to the CGI program. In the case of SEARCH.BAT, the program will search for the filename(s) the user typed in.

This is the most complex example we have looked at so far, and it may take a little work to master, but the principles are fairly straightforward. Here is how the program works, one section at a time:

Figure 4.4: *Search screen displayed by SEARCH.BAT.*

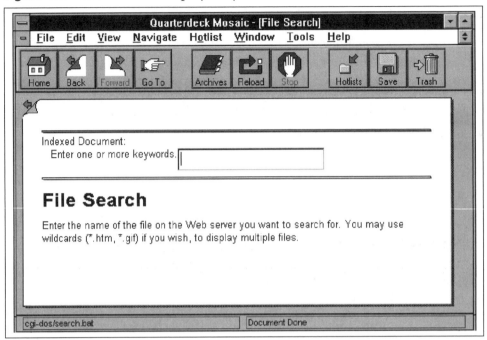

The first step is to send the Content-type header and a blank line (remember, the blank line is just as important as the header itself).

Next, the program looks to see if a parameter was passed to it:

```
if (%1)==() goto noargs
```

This line means "If there are no command-line arguments" (that is, you are running it for the first time) go to the *noargs* label and continue executing there." Therefore, when the program runs for the first time, the program will jump to the "noargs" section and output DIR1.TXT. This file contains directions to the user and the crucial <ISINDEX> tag, which tells the browser to put a query field on the page so the user can type in a parameter.

The user types in a parameter and runs the program a second time. This time, the IF line will find a parameter, so instead of jumping to the "noargs" label, the batch file just continues with the next line, labeled "args". SEARCH now executes three commands, redirecting and appending the output of each to %OUTPUT_FILE% (Figure 4.5):

- First, TYPE DIR2.TXT, which sends HTML heading material to the output file.
- Next, the DIR /S command searches for the requested files (the other command parameters format the DIR command output).
- Finally, TYPE DIR3.TXT, which sends the closing HTML code to the output file.

Figure 4.5: *Results of entering the search string *.GIF in SEARCH.BAT.*

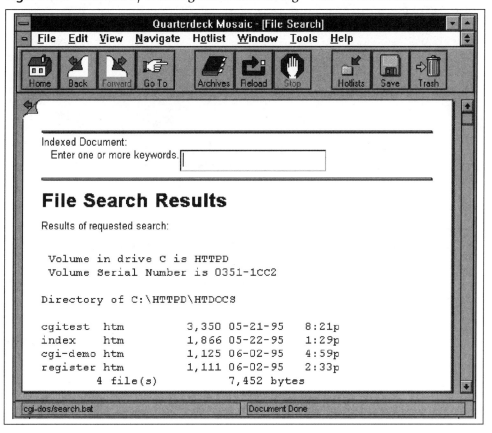

Here is the complete source for SEARCH.BAT:

```
echo Content-type: text/html >%output_file%
echo. >>%output_file%
if (%1)==() goto noargs
:args
type c:\httpd\cgi-bin\dos\dir2.txt >>%output_file%
dir c:\httpd\htdocs\%1 /-p/-w/l/s >>%output_file%
type c:\httpd\cgi-bin\dos\dir3.txt >>%output_file%
goto end
:noargs
type c:\httpd\cgi-bin\dos\dir1.txt >>%output_file%
goto end
:end
```

DIR1.TXT contains an HTML file which is displayed the first time SEARCH.BAT is run:

```
<HTML>
<HEAD>
<TITLE>File Search</TITLE>
<ISINDEX>
</HEAD>
<BODY>
<H1>File Search</H1>
Enter the name of the file on the Web server
you want to search for.
You may use wildcards (*.htm, *.gif) if you wish, to display
multiple files.
</BODY></HTML>
```

DIR2.TXT contains the top of the HTML document: the opening <HTML> tag, the document title, a heading, and some formatting commands:

```
<HTML>
<HEAD>
<TITLE>File Search</TITLE>
<ISINDEX>
</HEAD>
<BODY>
<H1>File Search Results</H1>
```

```
<P>Results of requested search:
<PRE>
```

DIR3.TXT contains commands which close the formatting begun in DIR2.TXT, and two commands that conclude the HTML file:

```
</PRE>
</BODY>
</HTML>
```

Writing Windows-based Scripts with Visual Basic

As you can see from SEARCH.BAT, there are definite limits to what can be done with DOS batch files. DOS does have its uses, but for CGI, it presents many problems.

As you saw above, DOS batch files necessitate rather inelegant methods for creating HTML files. There is also a crucial technical limitation: when Windows runs a DOS application, it creates a "virtual machine" that requires significantly more time and system resources than a native Windows application would. We unconditionally recommend Windows-based programming languages to create CGI applications.

One of the easiest Windows programming languages is Visual Basic. The Visual Basic CGI interface is slightly more complicated than the DOS interface, but we have included a Visual Basic program—CGI.BAS, which you will find in the CGI-SRC/WIN directory—that does all the work behind the scenes. It collects environment variables, opens output files, and much more.

To use CGI.BAS, you simply add it to your project and use the subroutine CGI_Main (a routine supplied in CGI.BAS).

To get the feeling for creating a CGI Visual Basic program, here is an advanced version of HELLO.EXE, written in Visual Basic:

```
Sub CGI_Main ()
    Send "Content-type: text/html"
    Send ""
    Send "<html>"
    Send ""
```

```
      Send "<head>"
      Send ""
      Send "<title>Hello Program</title>"
      Send ""
      Send "</head>"
      Send ""
      Send "<body>"
      Send ""
      Send "<h1>Hello, World Wide Web</h1>"
      Send ""
      Send "<hr>"
      Send ""
      Send "<h2>With VB, we can send <i>formatted</i> text!"
      Send "<br>Here is an example of character formatting:
          </h2>"
      Send "<hr>"
      Send "<br>This is normal."
      Send "<br><b>This is bold.</b>"
      Send "<br><i>This is italics.</i>"
      Send "<pre>This is fixed pitch.</pre>"
      Send "<h2>And here are headings:</h2>"
      Send "<hr>"
      Send "<h1>This is text in heading 1 style</h1>"
      Send "<h2>This is text in heading 2 style</h2>"
      Send "<h3>This is text in heading 3 style</h3>"
      Send "<h4>This is text in heading 4 style</h4>"
      Send "<h5>This is text in heading 5 style</h5>"
      Send "<h6>This is text in heading 6 style</h6>"
      Send "</body>"
      Send ""
      Send "</html>"
   End Sub
```

Notice how simple this is: To put an HTML command in the output, you just use the "Send" function (which is defined for you in CGI.BAS). You can build an entire HTML file quickly and easily one line at a time with "Send." Figure 4.6 shows the output of this program.

Forms

Forms are one of the most powerful features HTML provides. Your HTML form is displayed by the browser as a page with fill-in fields, buttons, or other controls. When the user fills out the form and submits it (usually

Figure 4.6: *The output of the Visual Basic "Hello" program.*

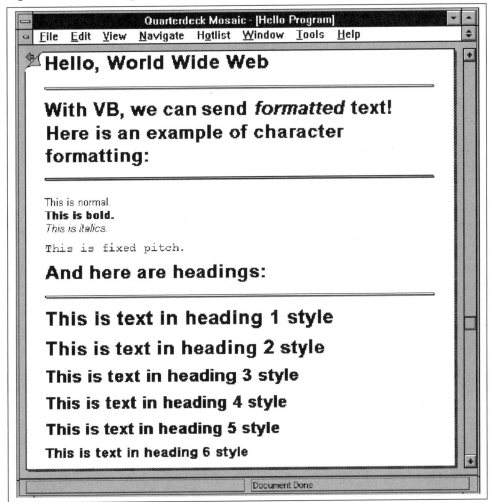

by clicking on a Submit button), the values entered into the form are passed to your CGI program for processing.

Before discussing the controls a form can contain, however, we need to cover the Form tag itself. An HTML Form tag looks something like this:

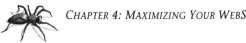

```
<FORM METHOD="post" ACTION="/cgi-win/program.exe">
(form elements go here)
</FORM>
```

The METHOD attribute determines how the data the user enters will be sent to the server. As a rule, use POST unless you have a good reason to use its alternative, GET (consult an HTML reference for more information on form options). The second attribute, ACTION, is the name of the CGI program the server should run to process the form data. Following the opening form tag are the form controls, which provide means for the user to enter his or her data. The form ends with a </**FORM**> closing tag.

Common Form Controls

Here is a look at the most common form controls.

Single-Line Text Box

To create a single-line text box, you use the Input tag with the input type "text." You must specify a variable name. Optionally, you can specify default text with the "default" attribute.

```
<INPUT TYPE = "text" NAME ="variablename" MAXLENGTH=number>
```

Textarea

Use <**TEXTAREA**> for larger text blocks. Row and Column attributes determine the size of the text block. You can optionally specify default text.

```
<TEXTAREA NAME="variablename", ROWS=number, COLUMN=number>Default
values go here</TEXTAREA>
```

Radio Buttons

Radio buttons come in groups; they permit you to select one option only.

```
<INPUT TYPE = "radio" NAME = "variablename" VALUE="Button 1">Button 1
<INPUT TYPE = "radio" NAME = "variablename" VALUE="Button 2">Button 2
<INPUT TYPE = "radio" NAME = "variablename" VALUE="Button 3">Button 3
```

Checkbox Buttons

Checkboxes come in groups like radio buttons, but you can select any number of items.

```
<INPUT TYPE="checkbox" NAME="variablename"
VALUE="Button 1">Button 1
<INPUT TYPE="checkbox" NAME="variablename"
VALUE="Button 2">Button 2
<INPUT TYPE="checkbox" name="variablename"
VALUE="Button 3">Button 3
```

Combo Boxes

Combo boxes (also sometimes called "list boxes") use the <SELECT> tag, followed by a list of options.

```
<SELECT NAME="variablename">
<OPTION SELECTED>Option 1
<OPTION>Option 2
<OPTION>Option 3
<OPTION>Option 4
</SELECT>
```

Submit Button

The form's **Submit** button works like the **OK** button in most dialog boxes. The button text can say "Submit," or you can use the VALUE attribute to substitute your own text.

```
<INPUT TYPE = "submit" VALUE="Optional Button Text")
```

Reset Button

The **Reset** button is similar to the **Cancel** button in most dialog boxes, but instead of dismissing the dialog box, it clears all the values entered so far.

```
<INPUT TYPE="reset" VALUE="Optional Button Text">
```

Forms and Windows Scripts: Sample Application

An HTML page follows that uses most of these form elements: a registration form you might employ for users signing up for some product or service. Figure 4.7 shows the output of this code.

```
<HTML>
<HEAD>
<TITLE>Form Program</TITLE>
</HEAD>
<BODY>
<H2>Register With Us!</H2>
<FORM METHOD="post" ACTION="/cgi-win/newuser.exe">
<HR>
<PRE>
First Name:     <INPUT TYPE="text"     NAME="FirstName"
    MAXLENGTH="24"  SIZE="24">
Last Name:      <INPUT TYPE="text"     NAME="LastName"
    MAXLENGTH="24"           SIZE="24">
Password:       <INPUT TYPE="password" NAME="Password"
    MAXLENGTH="12"           SIZE="12">
E-mail Address: <INPUT TYPE="text"     NAME="Email"
    MAXLENGTH="50" VALUE = "" SIZE="50">
Operating System: <SELECT NAME="OperatingSystem">
<OPTION SELECTED>Windows
<OPTION>DOS
<OPTION>Macintosh
<OPTION>Unix
</SELECT>
Sex:
    <INPUT TYPE="radio" NAME="Sex" VALUE="Male">Male
    <INPUT TYPE="radio" NAME="Sex" VALUE="Female">Female
I use my computer at:
    <INPUT TYPE="checkbox" NAME="WhereUse" VALUE="Home">Home
    <INPUT TYPE="checkbox" NAME="WhereUse" VALUE="Work">Work
    <INPUT TYPE="checkbox" NAME="WhereUse"
        VALUE="School">School
<INPUT TYPE="submit" VALUE="Register!"> <INPUT TYPE="reset"
    VALUE="Start Over">
</PRE>
</FORM>
<HR>
</BODY>
</HTML>
```

Figure 4.7: *The sample form displayed in a browser.*

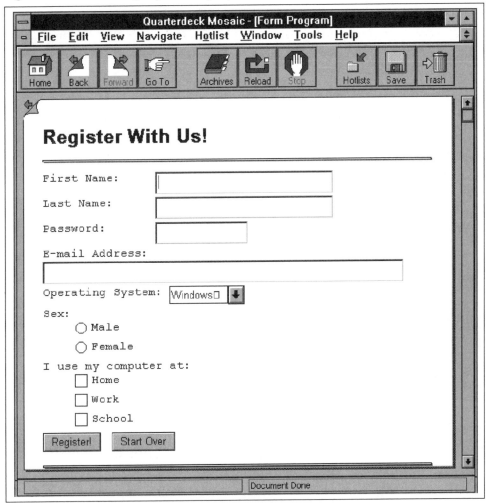

How do we handle the information returned when the user presses the **Register** button? With Visual Basic and the supplied CGI.BAS program, it is surprisingly easy. Here's the CGI_Main core of REGISTER.EXE, the script called by the sample form:

```
Sub CGI_Main ()
    Dim i As Integer
    Send "content-type: text/html"
    Send ""
```

```
Send "<html>"
Send "<head>"
Send "<title>Form Program</title>"
Send "</head>"
Send "<body>"
Send "<h1>Form Registration Example</h1>"
Send "<hr>"
Send ("<h2>Here are the values you entered:</h2>")
If CGI_NumFormTuples > 0 Then
    Send ("<ul>")
    For i = 0 To CGI_NumFormTuples - 1
        Send ("<li><b>" & CGI_FormTuples(i).key & ":
            </b>" & CGI_FormTuples(i).Value)
    Next i
    Send ("</ul>")
Else
    Send ("(none)")
End If
Send ("<hr>")
Send "</body>"
Send "</html>"
End Sub
```

The heart of the program is the loop:

```
For i = 0 To CGI_NumFormTuples - 1
    Send ("<li><b>" & CGI_FormTuples(i).key & ": </b>" &
            CGI_FormTuples(i).Value)
Next i
```

CGI_NumFormTuples is a variable that contains the number of elements on our page. These elements are passed to our program in pairs, called key/value pairs. The key is the variable name and the value is the variable's value. For example, for a text input field defined as

```
<INPUT TYPE="text" NAME="FirstName" MAXLENGTH="24"  SIZE="24">
```

the key is FirstName, and if the user enters "Mike" into this field on the form, the value of FirstName is "Mike."

These key/value pairs are stored in an array of records called CGI_FormTuples, with each record holding one key/value pair. So CGI_FormTuples(0).key holds the first key and CGI_FormTuples(0).Value holds the first value. The loop simply looks at how many key/value pairs there are and, for each one, displays the key followed by the value. In a real application, you would probably pass this information to a database program for storage. Note that some browsers may pass this information in reverse order, so check each key string before you assume what it is.

Figure 4.8: *The output of REGISTER.EXE.*

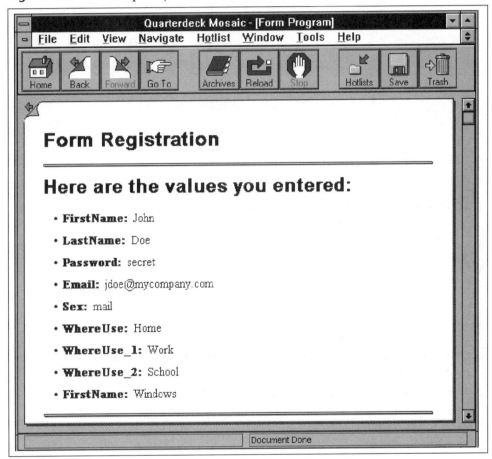

Imagemaps

Like the previous examples, imagemaps are CGI programs, but the programming itself has already been done; the CGI program you use is called IMAGEMAP.EXE.

To create an imagemap, you take a GIF image, and map certain regions of the image to certain URLs. Then, when a user clicks on a region that you have mapped, the mapped URL is loaded.

Figure 4.9:   *An imagemap.*

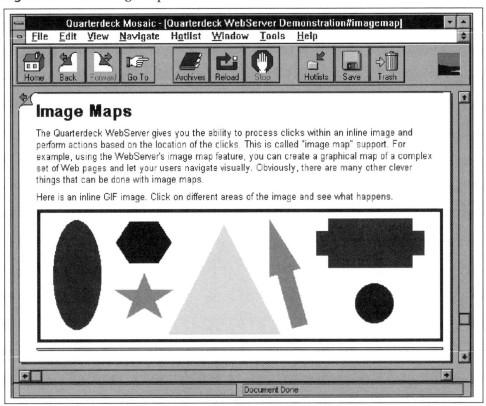

Here are the steps for creating a working imagemap:

1. Create an imagemap file for the image. Although some paint programs will give you the coordinates of regions in an image, the

easiest way to create an imagemap in Windows is with a program called Mapedit, which will generate map files for you. It is free for personal use, and you can find it at this URL:

```
ftp://sunsite.unc.edu/pub/packages/infosystems/WWW/tools/mapedit
```

This map file you create for an image usually bears the base name of the image plus a .map extension. An imagemap file simply lists the type of region, URL, and coordinates.

Here is the imagemap file for the image displayed in Figure 4.9. The "default" line lists a URL to call when the user clicks on part of the image that is undefined.

```
default /qdeck/immap.html
rect /index.html 16,13 111,40
rect /qdeck/web.html 16,41 112,65
rect /qdeck/qa.html 18,68 113,92
rect /qdeck/tools.html 18,94 113,120
rect /qdeck/writing.html 276,14 380,38
rect /qdeck/clients.html 276,41 381,64
rect /qdeck/founders.html 278,66 382,90
rect /qdeck/pub.htm 1279,93 382,122
default /error.html
rect /index.html 16, 13, 111, 40
rect /qdeck/web.html 16, 41, 112, 65
rect /qdeck/qa.html 18, 68, 113, 92
```

2. Put the map file in the directory reserved for imagemaps. In Quarterdeck WebServer, this is HTTPD/CONF/MAPS.

3. Choose an alias for the imagemap file (you can use the base name of the file) and put a mapping from the alias name to the filename in IMAGEMAP.CNF, which is found in the HTTPD/CONF directory.

4. Put the link to the imagemap in your HTML document, and use the attribute ISMAP in the IMG tag to indicate that the image is an imagemap rather than just a regular picture.

When the image is clicked, the server executes the CGI IMAGEMAP.EXE program, which comes installed with WebServer in your CGI-WIN directory. How does the IMAGEMAP.EXE program know which imagemap to use? You pass it a parameter with the map's name using the extra-path syntax, discussed earlier. This means you follow the name of the IMAGEMAP.EXE program with a slash and the name of the alias (which you should put in IMAGEMAP.CNF).

Here is a typical imagemap anchor reference:

```
<A HREF="/cgi-win/imagemap.exe/vrcloud4>
<IMG SRC="vrcloud4.gif" ISMAP></A>
```

There's a lot more we could go into about all this CGI nonsense. It's a really important part of making your Web site stand out. But it would require an entire book to do it justice. There is lots of information on the Internet itself about creating CGIs. Many of these places are included in Appendix F. Have fun and explore. It must be obvious by now that CGIs are not for the faint of heart. We've tried to give you a taste of what they can do. From here, you're on your own. In the next chapter, we'll get into ways of maximizing your server's performance. You may want to order a pizza before starting the next chapter—but don't get the pages messy.

Chapter 5

A LOOK AT NT WEB SERVERS

Bob & Jeff Go Windows Shopping

Here's the deal. It's time to start getting serious and you need to decide how far you're willing to go. There are two drawbacks to running your Web site with WebServer on a PC with Windows 3.1. The first drawback you can buy your way out of with money. The second one requires a change in lifestyle.

Issue Numero Uno: 16-Bit Ain't It

If you are married to setting your Web site up on a PC and want to be able to handle more than a few "hits" at a time on your server, you need to bite the bullet and say goodbye to Windows 3.1. It's time to upgrade your PC's operating system to Windows NT. It's going to cost you about $500 for the NT software. Believe us — you'll love it! Blow off Windows 95. If you like the new interface of 95, you can have it on NT too. The serious TCP/IP server stuff for the PC is being done on NT, and the TCP/IP that is built into NT is awesome. It's almost as easy to configure as a Mac (dare we say), and using it opens up all sorts of possibilities and choices when it comes to serving up content on the Internet.

The fact is, Windows 3.1 and the Web servers out there for it just can't handle the load. A Web site running on them starts choking and crashing when you reach about 12 to 16 simultaneous hits. NT, on the other hand, can handle boatloads of users visiting your site. Since NT is a multitasking and multithreaded operating system, the limit on the amount of traffic your server can handle is limited only by the amount of RAM and bandwidth you have. Performance-wise, it's much more like UNIX — without the added complexity.

You're also going to need to have at least 12 — and preferably 16 — megs of RAM on your CPU. You may already have the RAM if you've been running any Microsoft apps recently. Pop for NT. Buy the RAM if you need to. You'll be happy you did.

Issue Numero Dos: Nerd Alert Time!

The second issue you're soon going to run into when running a Web site on a PC is that you need to be comfortable with the idea that it's going to take some programming skills to do anything innovative with your Web site. Most of the CGIs that connect a page on your Web site to a backend app such as a Microsoft Access database require some knowledge of Visual Basic, PERL, or C programming.

There are several "canned" solutions that come with the Windows 3.1 packages that don't require knowing Visual Basic or having much knowledge in the way of programming — but even these are going to seem a little complicated to the uninitiated. It gets even more troublesome when you try to figure out what someone means when they say things like the Web server they run includes a reference implementation in Visual Basic that has a reusable module that creates the CGI environment within a VB program.

Yeah, right. Nerd alert! Nerd alert!

OK, some of you know what that means. We don't. We like our life-style and don't need to become any geekier than we already are — especially Jeff. If you don't believe us, take a look at that picture of him on the back of the book. It may be too late.

Issue Numero Tres: When to Upgrade or ...

Quarterdeck has done a great job writing the HTML-ized documentation that comes with their server. Take the time and read it. They cover every-thing thoroughly from setting up server stats and graphs to creating clickable imagemaps.

If you started your WebMaster career with Windows HTTPd, most of what you learned can be carried over to O'Reilly's WebSite when you make the leap to a more serious Web server. In fact, a lot of the WebSite setup is even easier. When you read through and try out all the goodies you'll get a good sense of how complicated your life may or not become as a Windows WebMaster. A lot depends on your motivation. Like every-thing else, it's an ever-expanding finite body of knowledge. The same will be true with a move to Quarterdeck's Windows 95 and NT solutions.

If you find the going easy, you're set. If you find it's overwhelmingly complicated, but you're still intent on setting up a Web site with all sorts of bells and whistles — face it — you're hosed. You need to either hire someone to help, hunker down and learn your way around the dark recesses of programming for Windows, or really do something com-pletely radical and buy a Mac and run the WebSTAR WWW server. You could even get a Mac OS clone like a Power Computing Power 100 (a shameless plug from Bob, their Chief Evangelist) and buy our *WebMaster Macintosh* book.

We live to ease your pain.

Remember, we're talking about what's required to set up a robust WWW site on a PC running Windows. You can stick with Windows http or WebServer and Windows 3.1 and blow off all the bells and whistles. You'll still have a great little site to publish on the Net with. Your pages will just be limited to some HTML and graphics and not much else. It's a great place to start but it won't take you everywhere you want to go.

Get NT. Get the RAM. Learn how to do some simple programming with Visual Basic and get with the program. Come on — go for it. You can do it. We had to.

NT Action

Windows NT is the real deal. Let's start with an overview of why it's so great. As soon as that's covered, we'll show you all the best WWW server software that is available for NT. You're going to have several options, and we're going to help you to make an informed decision. Microsoft has some excellent pages on its WWW site at **http://www. microsoft.com/BackOffice** that cover Windows NT. You can learn all the mumbo jumbo you want about the Windows NT Workstation and the Windows NT Server operating systems and why they are the best thing that Microsoft has done in years. There's both an NT Server and an NT Workstation operating system. Most of you will be happy running your Web site on the NT Workstation and will never require the type of network management and multiprotocol support that the NT Server offers. Besides that, you're better off parking your Web site on a dedicated machine than on a CPU running the NT server and handling printers, network routing, user accounts and permissions, and a whole host of other services.

By the way, while you're at the Microsoft WWW site, browse around the BackOffice pages a little. You'll get a really good feel for the direction Microsoft is heading with its operating systems and integrated suites of applications. Besides, they have a nice clickable imagemap.

A Quick Word about Windows 95

In case you've been dead and didn't know, Windows 95 is Microsoft's new 32-bit operating system. It's targeted at people who perform a variety of general tasks such as word processing, database queries, spreadsheet analysis, or who use applications that are specific to their particular business — in short, all those millions of Windows 3.1 users.

> ## A Quick Word about Windows 95 (continued)
>
> Windows 95 is the best choice for a business or individual using a PC who has an installed base of personal computers, peripheral devices and applications.
>
> Since you want to run a WWW server and maybe a few other Internet-accessible servers, such as an FTP site for your downloadable files, you couldn't care less. You need NT. Windows NT is the ideal Internet server solution for Windows WebMasters. The Windows NT Workstation and Server are designed to fully tap the capabilities of leading-edge hardware such as the RISC chip and multiprocessor configurations.
>
> You want NT for its performance and for the fact the there's more TCP/IP server software available and supported for NT than there is for 95. Microsoft runs all of their Internet servers on Windows NT, including ftp.microsoft.com, www.microsoft.com and gopher.microsoft.com.

Windows NT has all sorts of great things built right in such as an FTP server and client as well as Telnet client software. There's even an "Internet Toolchest" of free public domain NT Internet servers available that includes HTTP for Web, Gopher, WAIS, Mail and Finger. You can find them all at EMWAC — The European Microsoft Windows NT Academic Centre. The URL for EMWAC is:

http://emwac.ed.ac.uk

We recommend you take a look at the free NT WWW server from EMWAC. In fact, we've included it on the CD-ROM that came with this book so you wouldn't have to wait around for it to download from some FTP site. We went ahead and nabbed all the other free stuff for you too.

There's a big drawback to the EMWAC HTTPS Web server — besides the fact that it's a "do-it-yourself-figure-it-out-on-your-own-who-do-I-ask-for-help" piece of software. The EMWAC Web server doesn't support using Visual Basic as the programming language to write your CGIs in.

You have to do them in C or Perl. Neither does it support setting up security to restrict access to certain pages on your Web server.

Going the EMWAC route to set up a Web server is fine if you're already an expert. We assume that you're not an expert and want us to guide you through the mine fields.

Okay, so guide me already.

NT Apples and Bananas

Let's sort out the different NT Web server software options you have. As of this writing there are too many NT Web servers to mention. We think there are basically three of them to choose from:

- WebSite
- Purveyor
- Netscape NT server

Netscape Communications Corporation you know and love. As of September 1995 they had just released an NT Web server. Process Software Corporation sells Purveyor. It's the commercial version of the EMWAC HTTPS Web server. And WebSite is the Web server from O'Reilly & Associates, Inc. It's based on Robert Denny's Windows HTTPd and is also available for Windows 95. Quarterdeck should have an NT Web server soon, but as of this writing, it wasn't available.

You're going to pay for one of these Web servers, so you need to know a little about the price, features, benefits and support you can expect from each. We could have written 50 pages on this. But no. You're going to get something much more useful.

Our Recommendations

If you're reading this book and thinking about making the move to NT, we think you'll like WebSite the most. It has the nicest look and feel and is the easiest to configure. Our gut feeling is that O'Reilly's WebSite is targeted to users like those of you reading this book who are beginners to intermediate in skill and who recognize the value of running a Web server on NT.

We think that the Purveyor and Netscape NT Web servers are the way to go if you plan on running a big commercial operation on NT and want the peace of mind of knowing you bought an expensive $2000+ solution. Netscape has the marketing clout, obviously. They also have some stock we wished we owned when they went public! Netscape has the easier-to-administer server of the two big-ticket servers. Purveyor, on the other hand, comes from Process, a company that has been putting out TCP/IP solutions for years. Give them both a test drive and see which one you like best.

Don't write off WebSite just because someone told you that O'Reilly is a book publisher and not a software company. We're confident they will do a great job supporting WebSite. Everything about O'Reilly as a company is excellent. Support and future enhancements for WebSite will be no exception. All things being equal, if we had a choice of who to work for, it would definitely be O'Reilly. Besides having the best t-shirts, we've liked everyone we've ever met there.

Blow off the marketing noise and industry credentials that Netscape and Process are perceived to have. Once you've hit the envelope with Windows 3.1 solutions, we think you'll find WebSite the best value for performance.

We hope we weren't too wishy-washy trying to be nice to everyone. You get our drift. Take your time making the decision. Test drive all the NT servers like we did. That won't cost you anything. In the next chapter, we interview some of the leading figures of the Net. Among other insights, we'll get their opinions on the different Web servers.

Chapter 6

INTERVIEWS WITH THE GODS

The Best and Brightest Netheads Speak Their Minds

On the following pages you'll hear from several of the most influential Internet luminaries: Windows HTTPd and WebSite creator Robert Denny; Internet business and marketing author Jill Ellsworth; and the founder of City.Net, Kevin Altis. We plan to do interviews regularly on the WebMaster Windows WWW site at **http://www.webmasterwin.com** — be sure to visit.

Robert Denny (O'Reilly & Associates)

JEFF & BOB: You started off with Windows HTTPd and ended up over at O'Reilly with WebSite. Why the move?

ROBERT DENNY: The Windows 3.1 environment (and particularly the stability of the many TCP packages that are available) is not robust enough to support a commercial Web server product. This appears to have improved as of late, but it certainly was the situation last year.

In addition, I used the Windows HTTPd project as a learning experience, to find out what people's "real" needs were and where the support issues would be. After answering literally thousands of e-mail messages, and saving all of them, I had a tremendous base on which to design a second-generation server. By last fall, I had really gotten the itch to move on from my job as CEO of ALisa Systems, Inc. I founded ALisa and served as its CEO for 12 years. Deep down, though, I was, and always will be, a "software artist." So when Jay Weber introduced me to Dale Dougherty and we started talking about a commercial server, I was spring-loaded to go for it.

JEFF & BOB: Do you have any plans for Windows HTTPd?

ROBERT DENNY: I have released updates on about a 90-day cycle. The latest was at the beginning of June. I don't have any firm plans to add major features, just fix bugs and add minor features.

JEFF & BOB: What to you think about Quarterdeck's new product called WebServer?

ROBERT DENNY: I licensed Quarterdeck to use the Windows HTTPd sources as the basis of their server. Since then, they have added significant value. I haven't seen the final product, but I have a lot of respect for Bob Kutnick and Emerick Wood, who are heading up that effort. I'm confident that the product will be a good one.

JEFF & BOB: WebSite also runs on Windows 95. Is running a Web server on 95 really an option?

ROBERT DENNY: Certainly! It isn't the heavy-duty OS that NT is, but it supports light to moderate server activity (tens of thousands of transactions per day) without impacting your own use of the system.

JEFF & BOB: Why wouldn't you just do it on NT?

ROBERT DENNY: Money. NT takes 32MB of RAM to be an effective server and user machine, 95 will live okay on 16MB. Also, the Win95 UI is a lot nicer to use than the old ProgMan/FileMan UI of NT. Once they get the full "new UI" on NT, I definitely would use NT if I could afford the RAM. NT is a hell of an OS.

JEFF & BOB: Are there any other TCP/IP server apps in the works for 95?

ROBERT DENNY: There have been rumors, but we scooped the market with WebSite. There are rumors of others doing 95 servers....

JEFF & BOB: There are a ton of them for NT.

ROBERT DENNY: Well, not a ton of them—EMWAC, EMWAC/Pro, Purveyor, NetSite (new), ZBServer (16-bit) ...

JEFF & BOB: Does the TCP/IP development community consider 95 a way to go — and are they developing for it?

ROBERT DENNY: They should. If you are careful and test on both 95 and NT, you can build TCP apps that run on either using the same executable image. WebSite has shown itself to be the fastest of the NT servers, and it runs on 95 as well. So as you can see, no-compromise performance is achievable with a complex server app running on either platform.

JEFF & BOB: What about the hassle that nonprogrammers have doing CGIs on a PC? On the Mac there are a boatload of "out-of-the-box" CGIs that require very little modification. Are there any easy ways to implement CGIs in the works — say something that would hook a PC Web server into a Microsoft Access database?

ROBERT DENNY: There are several powerful CGI-based add-ons in the works. I can't say too much more ....

JEFF & BOB: Have you seen Hot Java? What do you think about the possibilities?

ROBERT DENNY: Interesting, but UNIX-centered at the moment. We'll see if this makes inroads.

JEFF & BOB: What excites you most about what's happening on the Net?

ROBERT DENNY: People are communicating with each other in new ways. Publishing has been turned upside down: It is now not "distribution," it is "access." I see this as potentially having as much impact as the Gutenberg Press did. The ninnies are certainly making the same sorts of noises they did in Gutenberg's days :-).

JEFF & BOB: Where do you hang out when you surf around?

ROBERT DENNY: Surf? Huh? I spend virtually all of my "free" Net time reading and answering e-mail, participating in the WWW Usenet confs. I even get a bit of exploring in from time to time.

Robert Denny
rdenny@netcom.com
http://website.ora.com

Jill Ellsworth (Author)

JEFF & BOB: Jill, you're a frequent guest speaker and Internet luminary. In fact, you wrote one of the very first Internet books called *The Internet Business Book* published by John Wiley and Sons. You've got a new one out about marketing on the Net. What's it about?

JILL ELLSWORTH: Yep, ours was the first book to tell people that business is okay on the Net, and here is how to do it right. *Marketing on the Internet: Multimedia Strategies for the World Wide Web* is about how businesses and entrepreneurs can effectively use the Web for marketing, PR and selling. A recent review from Computer Literacy said:

> This book has sensitivity and maturity about what marketing on the Web is really like, at its best. The message here is the value of content-rich Web pages and online information, and how to engage customers early in the interaction. Many, many examples of business home pages, highlighting what relationships and activities can develop from customers visiting the site. Explains how to make and refine your own Web pages, how to network and get links to relevant URLs. Explains browsers,

WWW resources, and sites with resources for marketing. Outlines the *many* elements that make an effective Web presence. From the start, this book is more organically in-tune with the online world and with the personality of the Web than many Internet Business books.

Whew — could not have said it better myself ;>

JEFF & BOB: How do you keep up with all the Net goings on? What are your favorite on- and offline sources for info?

JILL ELLSWORTH: Keeping up is very difficult. I subscribe to net-happenings (Gleason Sackman's list) to get a look each day at what is new and interesting. I also read the internet-marketing list (**listserv@popco.com**), which is where the marketers hang out. Then I read a number of the www and html newsgroups to keep up, and I also like Edupage.

I regularly — 3 to 4 times a week — use Yahoo and WebCrawler, etc., to search for things on the Web, business, etc. I use the SIFT netnews service from Stanford to search UseNet newsgroups using my personal profiles in marketing, Web, net cash, etc. Similarly, I subscribe to the Newshound service from the *San Jose Mercury* — I have several profiles that search for items in business, marketing, education, the Web, etc.

And of course, I surf ...

Offline, I read *The New York Times, Business Week, Byte* and *Internet World,* among others.

JEFF & BOB: What are your three most important tips for budding WebMasters and WebMistresses who want to get in the business of creating Web sites and an effective Internet presence for themselves and for clients?

JILL ELLSWORTH: 1. Do good work — worry about quality.
2. Surf, surf, surf — use your eye to be critical about what is working and what is not. Look for useful sites as well as visually compelling sites.

3. The Internet is good for person-to person communication and for creating, gathering and using information — make a Web presence that embodies those characteristics.

4. [OK, I know you asked for three, but] Pay attention to the customer — your business customers and the page users.

Also see my successful/unsuccessful characteristics, below.

JEFF & BOB: We know that the answer to this next question could either be a book or a one-word "it depends" answer, but here goes anyway. Give it a shot, Jill. Do you think a business is better off outsourcing the creation of an Internet presence or should they do it themselves? When and why?

JILL ELLSWORTH: Generally, despite the size of the business, I think a business is better off outsourcing. You get expertise and a professional approach, you have fewer security worries, and you get full services. Webmasters are professionals who can help businesses get the most from their efforts.

When outsourcing, it is of key importance to find someone collaborative — that will work with you to accomplish your business goals and won't always just say "Trust me, I know best."

Exceptions:

- individual startups who want to do all the HTML, etc. Even then I recommend working with a professional Web site provider.
- companies with in-house artistic, marketing, and computer-savvy people with sufficient hardware and software to pull it off. A rarity.

JEFF & BOB: What makes for a great WWW site? What are a few of your favorites and why?

JILL ELLSWORTH: Here are some points I make when I consult with business or do presentations on what makes for successful and unsuccessful Web sites.

- No Invisible Webs. The site is registered with all of the online search engines like Lycos, WebCrawler, InfoSeek, Tupilak, etc., and with the catalog listings such as EINet Galaxy, Yahoo, the Commercial Sites Index, etc. In addition, the registrations are kept up to date with new categories and new sites.

- No Dead Webs. The content is always fresh — no pages where no one has put any new information for months — avoid the ghost web.
- The site offers good content, content, content.
- The site has true value added: services, content, products, resources.
- The site maintainers are responsive —they answer queries and troubleshoot problems with links. No "404, URL not found" messages.
- The site has organizational and/or institutional support. The site is not set up by the guys "out back" where no one else in the organization knows anything about the site. The site has budget and personnel support.
- The site has good navigational design — it is intuitive as opposed to having the feeling that you are just wandering; it does not leave you out in cyberspace.
- The site is capable of gathering information about users through contests, newsletters, surveys, etc. You have given the user a good reason to give you information.
- The Web site is integrated with other marketing channels.
- The site has good design:
    - there are alternatives for images
    - interactivity with people is available
    - the site is sensible vs. "hot" —graphics, design, and colors are in synch with the corporate image
    - the site has consistent imagery and content from page to page

Unsuccessful pages also have some characteristics in common. Unsuccessful pages are:

- Invisible — you cannot find them in the haystack of the Web. The site has not been registered or listed.
- Neglected — no one answers the e-mail, no one takes care of the content or the links.
- The site is full of empty slogans and hype.

- The site is the only marketing channel.
- The site has no role in the business — not a priority.
- No one is responsible for the site — content and design are catch-as-catch-can.
- The site has poor design:
    - large, slow-loading graphics with no alternatives
    - navigation is unclear
    - "funny" URLs with lots of mixed cases and tildes
    - there are lots of one-way slogans with no chance for interactivity

I like:

- the FedEx site **<http://www.fedex.com>** — it is not flashy, it does not whirl and rotate, but it does something terrific —I can track my packages at any time.
- the Computer Literacy Site **<http://www.clbooks.com>** — it is clean, neat, functional, and lets me search and browse for books, and I do love books.
- the Southwest Airlines site **<http://www.iflyswa.com/>** — it is visually fun, and again lets me get useful information in a nifty format.
- the NSTN site **<http://www.nstn.ca>** — they have created an aesthetically pleasing environment that loads quickly, offers obvious navigation, and the search engine Tupilak.

For useful tools for WebMasters, I visit the WebMaster site frequently — useful stuff here **<http://gagme.wwa.com/~boba/masters1.html>**

JEFF & BOB: Do you think the whole Internet phenomenon will continue to grow at such an enormous rate — or will we be reading later this year in *Newsweek* that the whole notion of the Internet and electronic commerce is a bust?

JILL ELLSWORTH: RE: the Internet itself — it is the largest intentional community people have ever created — it is not going away. As a community, it is impossible to predict what it will look like in the future, but it is a community that exists because people want to communicate.

RE: electronic commerce — I believe that the Internet now is a little like TV was in the early 50s —bursting with promise and opportunities; I seriously doubt that it will develop as TV has, driven exclusively by commercial concerns. It supports entrepreneurs in ways that TV cannot approach. It *is* going to be a wild ride though! It's going to keep growing.

JEFF & BOB: What do you think about some of the evolving models for Net advertising? Now that sponsors are getting more sophisticated, they increasingly want to know what they're paying for. What do you think will become the most equitable way to charge for advertising?

JILL ELLSWORTH: I know that it will not be based on raw hits — that is nonsensical. I suspect we will develop some ways of creating rate cards based on site "readership" like TV and paper-based media have done. How many individual visitors did the site have, how long did they stay, which pages did they visit? The rate card would then be weighted on number of visitors, tempered by how long they stayed — the quick jump-in/jump-out visitor is worthless, whereas the dedicated browser is worth a great deal more.

Actually, I think sponsorship — paying for a whole package of things — will be the model as opposed to individual "spots" or ads. This will evolve, but I see it taking different paths than traditional advertising has taken.

JEFF & BOB: Any thoughts on what's new and exciting or where it's all headed? Give us a piece of that visionary thing and a hint of what to keep an eye out for.

JILL ELLSWORTH: Keep your eye on Java/Hot Java, virtual reality modeling, Internet video conferencing and swnrtpy. Applets are just right for the Internet — they permit quick creativity, individualization and interest — things that are valued by users.

VRML will make online life and commerce more fun, more "real" — imagine driving that car or picking up the vase. Group VRML will make education across the globe easy.

Video conferencing schemes of all kinds are coming on strong, and will allow us to use the Internet to see and hear one another.

And what, you say, is swnrtpy? It is the next killer app, and it is just around the corner, a gleam in someone's eye. I don't know what it is but I know it's coming, and I know it will surprise and delight us!

Jill Ellsworth
je@world.std.com

Kevin Altis (City.Net)

JEFF & BOB: Kevin, you worked on the development of proxy server technology with Lou Montulli (University of Kansas) and Ari Luotonen (CERN), who are both at NetScape Communication Corporation now. (A proxy server gives corporate users behind firewalls access to the Net and Web.) Then you left left Intel in November 1994 to pursue City.Net and to develop and market your own software tools for managing Web content. How did you get drawn in to the whole Web scene?

KEVIN ALTIS: I had been working on WWW technology since 1992, and I was attracted to the Web because I was trying to help our group at Intel to work a little smarter than other design groups. We had a basic problem in that we had multiple platforms (Supercomputers, RS6000s, SUN, Mac, Windows) without any applications that worked across all those platforms and just getting them to talk to each other to share a single file was tough, let alone sharing rich documents or any kind of groupware.

I had started looking at Gopher as a potential solution when I discovered the Web around the summer of 1992. Turned out I had excellent timing, because that's when the really interesting discussions started on the www-talk mailing list. XMosaic was version 0.8 or something like that and the first Windows browser, Cello, written by Thomas Bruce was still six months away.

JEFF & BOB: So HTML and the Net became the answer?

KEVIN ALTIS: The core idea was that via the Web, we could create inter-active content that was usable across all computing platforms, including handhelds, kiosks, television via game machines such as SEGA when TCP/IP cartridges came out, etc. Unlike print or television, where the content can only be viewed one way in the format it was created for, Web content could be used regardless of whether your screen is a TTY, b/w, color, 320x200, 640x480 or whatever. You could even create a text to speech Web browser for the blind or browse the Web via the phone with the right browser at the other end of the line. It also doesn't matter whether you have a modem or a T1 or a broadband connection, you can still reach 40,000 (whatever the latest total is) Web sites.

Even as the Web fragments over the next year with the introduction of PDF, OLE, OpenDoc, even more Netscape-specific extensions, etc., the core content that forms the basis of the Web will be cross-platform. We managed to go from a Web defined by XMosaic almost exclusively to the point where in less than a year Netscape represented 70% of the browsers in use, till now when Netscape market share is finally declining as 3 million AOL users come online and Microsoft readies their Windows 95 browser. I've logged over 100 different browsers at my site and the number goes up each week. Throughout the entire time, the VT-100 text-only browser Lynx has kept a 6 to 10% marketshare.

Also, it is important to remember that there is a Web architecture which allows each piece to develop somewhat independently of the other pieces. URLs can migrate to URNs, HTML is really HTML 1.0 (sort of), HTML 2.0, HTML 2.0 with Netscape extensions, HTML 3.0, HTTP is HTTP 0.9, HTTP 1.0, HTTP Proxies went from Tim's original Gateway idea to HTTP Proxies, which is now the standard method of getting through firewalls and formed the basis for caching on the web. While our existing interactive elements on the Web such as content negotia-tion in HTTP, imagemaps, and CGI are fairly primitive right now, people all over the world have done simply outstanding tricks from software upgrades to remotely controlled robots. Obviously the Web isn't limiting people's creativity too much.

JEFF & BOB: So you started City.Net to provide a place on the Net for people to find communities online?

KEVIN ALTIS: … and provide a place where multiple points of view could come together. In our broadcast society, less than ten companies define what we read, hear, and watch. The basis for their material is largely driven by press releases and other forms of marketing such as the spin doctors of D.C. While I don't expect business as usual to change anytime soon, I do think that by starting to remove some of the barriers of communication on a mass scale such as capital requirements, print production, transportation of content, limited access to the airwaves, etc., more people will share their ideas and opinions.

We still don't know what the economics of this new decentralized and distributed medium are like, but the "media monopoly" was in need of a shakeup, and they're getting a good one.

JEFF & BOB: How many cities are on it now? How many visits does **http://www.city.net** get a week?

KEVIN ALTIS: 741 cities as of yesterday. We get around 50 site registrations a day and add about 25 cities a week. City.Net is visited by over 12,000 unique hosts a day with a 5% or so growth rate per week.

JEFF & BOB: Is this a labor of love, or are you getting financial support for it?

KEVIN ALTIS: Both. Commercial in that my company, City Net Express, is running City.Net. We're currently in the mode of a publisher and, based on the publishing industry norm, it might be two years before we're profitable based solely on advertising. However, we have a number of plans which will be implemented later this year and leverage off the popularity of City.Net, which hopefully will continue to support its growth.

JEFF & BOB: Where do you think that whole scene is headed? Is the Net just going to be one billboard after another at the beginning of each Web page?

KEVIN ALTIS: It seems like the Web spots that get the most press are the ones with the eye candy, but that's what you would expect. Our own breakdown of sites favors the ones that are content-rich or provide a unique point of view. The best ones are typically labors of love with little eye candy, but they're the ones you go back to again and again. If consumers lean toward glitz over substance then we might be headed for a Hollywood TV nightmare, but right now I think it is more likely the Net will adopt the economics of the print industry.

Do you support yourself by writing? Do you expect your book to pay your salary this year? How many people, companies will make money off your publication and what's the ratio for each? Forget about 500 channels, we get 500 new sites a week. One thing the Web is showing us is how advertising and content reimbursement will have to change as audience share is divided up more and more and the concept of content for 1,000 people or 10,000 people becomes the norm.

JEFF & BOB: How about the future? You've seen Hot Java, right? What do you think of it? Have you checked out the NandO Times site?

KEVIN ALTIS: Nobody actually uses Hot Java. OLE and OpenDoc web work over the next six months will give a better idea of where browsers are going. NandO is pretty good. I don't actually use it myself, since most of it is not applicable to my area, but I think it is a good experiment in content. However, I seriously doubt it is paying for itself right now, so it would be interesting to get opinions directly from them. I suspect we're destined for more and more discussion groups off of base news, weather, and sports content but it will be a while before a production formula appears.

JEFF & BOB: Any thoughts about VRML? You think we're going to be able to do a Neuromancer thing to one of the links on City.Net anytime soon?

KEVIN ALTIS: I think VRML is actually sort of lame. The main thing for me right now is to keep the click-wait-watch latency as short as possible. I do think we'll see more elaborate environments built around something DOOM or Marathon or something new pretty soon. When you talk about zipping around links you have to wonder — why bother? A simulation of moving between two geographical locations would *just* be a simulation, since there is not actually anything between source and destination and the simulation would just increase the delay in movement.

Even doing a decent simulation would require an elaborate map of the network environment, which is way beyond anything we can do today and gets worse every hour. I've actually never understood how you could get to the Neuromancer or Snow Crash virtual world based on our reality of today. Gibson doesn't even use his computer for anything except word processing, so it isn't like the idea has any technical basis. If you can describe how it would be done, I would love to hear it since it has stumped me for over 10 years.

Kevin Altis
altis@home.city.net

Ed Tittel (Author and Networking Consulting)

JEFF & BOB: Do you think the whole scene is going to keep on keeping on at this breakneck pace?

ED TITTEL: I agree that the Web has been exploding in growth and use, especially in the last year. If anything, I see things getting even crazier in the near term, as Web presences for individuals and business become more the norm than they are today.

JEFF & BOB: What excites you the most about the Net and the possibilities that Net access creates?

ED TITTEL: Tim Berners-Lee indicated that the Web was capable of delivering the "sum of human knowledge and experience" in his initial architectural papers that defined the World Wide Web. In a larger sense, the same thing is true of the Internet as a whole: it's a way of bringing human knowledge and experience together, and of delivering it to anyone who knows how to ask for it — that's never been available before. To me, the most exciting thing about the Net is the availability of information on any topic, at almost any level of detail, any time I (or anybody else) wants it. It's changed the way I work and live, and has the potential to do that for most people. I see it creating a world where inequities imposed by location and background can be eliminated, and where expertise is defined as much by drive and passion as it is by formal training and credentials. This has the potential of creating a highly educated, highly egalitarian world where the people with the information and the insight can make things happen. In short, it sounds pretty good to me!

JEFF & BOB: It seems there's a new Web server coming out every day for the PC. Most of them are for NT. What turns you on about NT and serving up the IP services like WWW and FTP on it?

ED TITTEL: NT Server, and its Internet and IP tools, appears poised to make Internet services readily accessible to anybody who wants to take the time to learn how to use them. In the past, high barriers to entry barred most businesses and individuals from mounting their own presences on the Internet:

Barrier # 1: The high cost of a direct Internet connection. In the past, high-bandwidth digital communications was prohibitively expensive, and could block most smaller operations from shouldering the costs necessary to establish a true digital link to the Internet. The recent proliferation of ISDN, and the reduction in costs for Switched 56 and similar services from the telecomm companies, has suddenly made a dedicated, medium-sized pipe to the Internet affordable.

Barrier # 2: Entry into UNIX guru-hood. In the past, UNIX was the platform of choice for Internet services and access. Unfortunately, UNIX could be the operational definition of "arcane" and "complex," when it comes to operating systems. But the introduction of GUI software for end users, and operating systems like NT Server for the back-end, has suddenly made it easy and affordable for companies and individuals to establish a presence on the Internet.

Barrier # 3: Access to affordable IP services software. The same forces that kept UNIX the private preserve of a computing elite also helped to keep IP service applications expensive and hard to deal with: a small, tightly knit community of highly technical people interested in serving each other's needs, but only marginally interested in commercial concerns or in making the technology broadly available to all comers. The explosion of the Web and the Net, and the delivery of quality IP services software for platforms like the Macintosh and NT have really helped to popularize this technology, partly by demystifying it and making it easier to use, and partly by making it far more affordable than it's ever been before.

Given all this explanation, here's a short answer to this question: What turns me on is that lots of affordable, easy-to-use options are suddenly available, and now providing Internet access and services to all kinds of information and services collections is possible that otherwise never could have happened.

Jeff & Bob: A couple of problems a lot of people run into with their PCs is getting their Ethernet cards working properly with TCP/IP or getting their Net connections all set up and running smoothly. It seems it's way more complicated than it needs to be. Any suggestions on the best places to turn for help? There are so many different combinations of cards, CPUs, drivers and so on … how do you make sense of it all? We've always had a friend handy or just called someone up and paid them boatloads to figure it out. Can we do any better than that? Help us be more self-sufficient, Ed. Where are some good sources of info for everyone?

Ed Tittel: As an author of numerous books, I have a bit of an ax to grind here, but I happen to think that books, magazines, and online information resources offer a one–two–three combination that makes it possible to resolve most information problems. When it comes to IP and related networking or communications issues, I've found the books from a couple of publishers in particular to be extremely helpful:

1. If IDG offers a *Dummies* book on the subject I'm interested in, I'll start there to get oriented and to learn basic concepts and terminology.

2. After that, I look for detailed books from a variety of computer trade book publishers to help me out. I've had good luck with titles from IDG, Macmillan, AP Professional, and Addison-Wesley in looking for help.

3. I read most of the networking and computer trade magazines pretty regularly. I find that *Internet World, NetGuide,* and *IWAY* are useful sources of information about what's happening on the Internet, and that *Wired* is a great source of information about stuff that's a little over the bleeding edge of Internet thinking and technology.

I also get a lot of useful information from the mailing lists and newsgroups that I follow online. For the late-breaking news, and latest developments, these resources are hard to beat. FYI, I follow the various **comp.infosystems.www** newsgroups for Web information, I follow the various Novell and NetWare newsgroups, and I subscribe to the HTML Working Group and the Netscape mailing lists. This results in about an extra 200 to 250 messages a day, so I can't say I read them all with deep attention, but I do look at all of them and pay attention to the stuff that interests me.

When it comes to nitty-gritty details of installation and configuration, knowing the underlying terminology and technology is about as far as books or magazines can get you. When you're dealing with this level of detail, technical support is the name of the game. When I get stumped with these kinds of issues, here's what I do:

1. I check the FAQs for the vendors or the products I'm having problems with.

2. I read the message traffic on the UseNet newsgroups that cover the relevant products or technologies, and look for common symptoms or complaints.

3. If I find them, I contact the authors of the original messages, and see what they've been able to learn, or if they've come up with any usable workarounds.

4. I'll check with the vendor (usually to see if they have an FTP site or a home page), and browse the available information resources. If there's a patch or a fix, I can usually find it and download it faster than calling technical support.

5. Only as a last resort do I ever call tech support. I hate living on hold, and often find that technical support operations don't have their first-line people fully in the know about recent developments. I've found myself telling them about new developments or enhancements rather than vice-versa on several occasions. But if you're really in a jam, and have the patience to wait for information, tech support can sometimes be a real life-saver.

Jeff & Bob: Besides answering your e-mail, what are you using the WWW and Net for, Ed? Do you ever just kick back and surf around? What are some of your favorite sites?

Ed Tittel: I use the WWW regularly for personal matters, as well as for researching books, articles, and consulting work. I spend at least 40 hours a week online, sometimes a great deal more, and use the WWW pretty much every chance I get. Outside of work-related stuff, we've used it recently to find out what my stepson's going to need at SMU to get online when he goes to school there this fall, to obtain information about some mountain bikes we might be buying, and to check prices on a few consumer items I'd rather not mention here.

I probably spend about 6 to 10 hours a week cruising the Web, just looking for cool stuff or fooling around. Lately, I've been most partial to Yahoo (**http://www.yahoo.com**) as my search engine, I've been fooling around with "WAX, or the discovery of television among the bees" (**http://bug.village.virginia.edu**), and have visited the SMU Website repeatedly (**http://smu.edu**). Other than that, I spend a fair amount of time in the alt.<whatever> hierarchy, particularly on the wine and cooking newsgroups, both of which I enjoy immensely (i.e., alt.food and its subgroups, especially alt.food.wine).

JEFF & BOB: What are you working on now? Any big projects you can tell us about?

ED TITTEL: I just finished a book on CGI programming for IDG books, called *The Foundations of WWW Programming, with HTML and CGI,* with Mark Gaither, Sebastian Hassinger, and Mike Erwin. Together, this same team is working on books on VRML and Java, with a *Web Programming Secrets* book also in the offing for IDG. At the same time, I'm working with Bob LeVitus on *Making Your CD-ROM Work* for Random Books, and a reprise of one of our favorite projects ever: *New and Improved Stupid Windows Tricks* for AP Professional. It's safe to say I'm seldom bored or idle!

Ed Tittel
etittel@zilker.net

Appendix A

GLOSSARY

Anchor(s)
The place(s) in an HTML document where a hypertext link(s) occurs.

Application
Software that performs a task or tasks. Usually a launchable program. Examples: a Web browser or word processor.

Application Layer
The OSI Reference Model layer that provides protocols for various network applications, such as eMail or file transfer.

Archie
A search protocol by which many of the FTP sites on the Internet can be examined simultaneously for files whose names match arbitrary patterns: you can search for files whether you know all or just a part of the filename.

ARPAnet
A 1970s experimental network that fostered the early development of Internet software.

Asynchronous Communication
Data transmission in which characters are sent one at a time, encapsulated in control bits. Also refers to commands which may be sent before a response to a previously sent command has been received.

Attributes
SGML (and HTML) tags may accept attributes that further define their usage (much as parameters are used with command-line options, for those of you lucky enough to be familiar with the good old command line). A tag is often followed by an attribute, which in turn is assigned a particular value.

Backbone Network
A network acting as a primary conduit for traffic that is often both sourced from, and destined for, other networks.

Bandwidth
A measure of the information-carrying capacity of a network, measured in bits per second. The greater the bandwidth, the greater the data transmission capacity of the network.

Baud
The number of times per second that a modem changes the signal it sends during data transmission. *See* Bits per second.

BinHex
A file conversion procedure used to convert binary files to ASCII text files and back again. Files are BinHexed before being transmitted via FTP or as attachments to eMail.

Bits per second (bps)
The rate of bit transmission over a communications link.

BRI
Basic Rate Interface is an ISDN service that has two full-duplex, 64 kbps B channels for data and voice transmissions and one full-duplex, 16 kbps D channel for control and monitoring functions. BRI is often referred to symbolically as "2B+D" or as "basic."

Browser
See Web browser.

BTW
A common eMail abbreviation for "by the way."

Cache
The process of storing data in select locations within memory for convenient retrieval.

CERN
The European Particle Physics Laboratory in Geneva, Switzerland. Their research on hypertext technology formed the basis for the World Wide Web.

CGI (Common Gateway Interface)
CGI is the standard for external gateway programs to interface with information servers such as HTTP servers.

CIX (Commercial Internet Exchange)
An organization founded to create an understanding between network providers regarding commercial traffic accounting methods.

Client

A computer that links to a server, utilizing the services it provides through a communication link.

Client–Server Architecture

The client–server relationship operates by having a client computer connect to a host (server) computer via its server program. The client connects to the server and transmits a request for information. The server then disconnects from the client, processes the information request, and reconnects to the client to deliver the result.

Cyberspace

A term commonly used to describe the Internet, probably coined by science fiction writer William Gibson.

Dedicated Line

A private telephone line reserved for a communication link between locations. For example, the connection between a LAN and an Internet provider will typically run on a dedicated line.

Dial-up Connection

The most common type of connection to the Net for home computer users, utilizing telephone lines to connect the host to an Internet-connected computer.

Direct Connection

A permanent connection between a single computer (or LAN) and the Internet, sometimes referred to as a "leased line connection."

Document

In World Wide Web parlance, a document refers to any text, media, or hyperlink file that can be transmitted to a client from an HTTP server.

Document Window
Commonly refers to the scrollable window in a client program in which HTML documents can be viewed.

DNS
The Domain Name System; a database tool that allows one to translate alphabetic computer names into Internet numeric addresses, freeing the Internet user from having to remember long lists of numbers.

Driver
Software that allows a peripheral or internal device to be used by a computer, such as an Ethernet card driver.

Electronic Mail (eMail, EMail, e-mail, etc.)
The transmission of information, usually text messages, between users over various types of networks, allowing for personalized addressing and other options, such as binary file (i.e., programs, documents) transfer with the message. *See* Eudora.

Enterprise Computing
A large computer network typically linking a variety of locations operating under various protocols within a large corporation.

EtherTalk
AppleTalk protocols running over Ethernet.

Eudora
An eMail program that operates over a TCP connection, originally developed by Steve Dorner at the University of Illinois. Freeware version is available from **http://www.qualcomm.com/quest/QuestMain.html**.

External Viewer
A "helper" application — a program that allows graphics, audio, or movies to be displayed in conjunction with or via a Web browser.

E-zines

Typically small, do-it-yourself publications that are distributed electronically over computer networks. For more info, go to **http://www.acns.nwu.edu/ezines/)**

FAQs/FAQ List (Frequently Asked Questions)

Internet text files that address common questions about a specific subject area, a handy source of Net knowledge typically maintained by UseNet newsgroups.

File Server

A computer on a network used specifically to store files that may be accessed and used by other computers on the network. A file server will often be "dedicated," meaning that it exists only for this purpose and is not used for any other tasks.

Firewall

See Security firewall.

Flame

A response to a UseNet post, usually in the form of a personal attack against the author or subject.

Frame

A group of information "bytes" transmitted over a data link, similar to a "packet."

Freenet

A provider of free Internet access to the public.

FTP (File Transfer Protocol)

A standard protocol used to transfer files from one computer to another, or the act of transferring files (using FTP).

FYI
An information sheet about the Internet, or a common eMail abbreviation meaning "for your information."

Gateway
A computer system that allows for the transfer of data between incompatible applications by reformatting the data before sending it to its destination.

GIF (Graphic Interchange Format)
A file compression format allowing transfer of graphics files through online services.

Gopher
A menu-driven tool (program) used to locate and link to online sources of information.

Gopherserver
A server configured to offer Gopher information.

Gopherspace
A term used to describe the entire Internet Gopher network.

Groupware
Applications designed to address tasks that involve two or more members of a group, such as meeting scheduling.

Helper Applications
See External viewers.

History
A function of some Web browsers that tracks all the documents viewed during the current session and allows you to call them up again.

Hits
Web slang for the number of visits tracked by a program like WebStat. More is usually better.

Home Page
The initial display on a Web site, through which one can access the other documents within the site.

Host
Typically, a computer that provides resources to other computers (clients) that reach it through a communications link, such as an Internet host computer.

Hotlist
A compilation, commonly personalized, of frequently visited Web sites and URLs.

HoTMetaL
A SoftQuad program that uses HTML codes to format documents for use on a Web site.

HTML (HyperText Markup Language)
A formatting language that instructs a Web browser on how to display a document's various components.

HTML Document
A document labeled in the HTML format, that may also be referred to as a Web document if it is accessible to the World Wide Web.

HTTP Server (Hypertext Transport Protocol)
A server computer that utilizes the communication protocol for Web document transfer.

Hyperlink
See Links.

Hypermedia
Graphics, movies, and audio features linked to a document, using the same principles as hypertext links.

Hypertext
Refers to a method of linking documents within a Web site that allows the browser to jump back and forth between files by clicking on hypertext "links."

IETF
See Internet Engineering Task Force.

IMHO
A common eMail or "chat" abbreviation for "in my humble opinion."

Inline Images
Graphics placed in a Web document that can either be loaded automatically, or by clicking on an icon.

Internet Architecture Board (IAB)
The group that makes decisions about standards and other important issues.

Internet Engineering Task Force (IETF)
A panel of volunteers that investigates and solves technical problems, and reports to the Internet Architecture Board.

Internet Resources
Information available to the public via the Internet.

Internet Service Provider (ISP)
An organization that provides Internet connections to its clients.

IP
"Internet Protocol." The most vital set of protocols that determine the way in which data travels across multiple networks via the Internet. IP is the network addressing portion of the TCP/IP protocol stack.

IP Address
An IP address is a number assigned to any Internet-connected computer.

IPX (Internet Packet Exchange)
A Novell NetWare protocol for transmitting and routing packets.

IRC (Internet Relay Chat)
Basically a huge multiuser live chat on the Internet. Chats can be public or private. There are a number of major IRC servers around the world which are linked to each other.

ISDN (Integrated Services Digital Network)
Communication protocols for the transfer of voice, data, and other media over telephone networks. Much, much faster than your v.34 modem.

ISP
See Internet Service Provider.

JPEG (Joint Photographic Experts Group)
An image compression protocol used to assist in the transfer of color images among computer networks.

LAN
See Local area network.

Layer
One set of network protocols that is part of a complete set of protocols.

Leased Line
See Dedicated line.

Links
Encoded text that allows you to jump from document to document in the Web. Also called hyperlinks, hotlinks, or anchors.

Linked Image
See Inline Images.

Local Area Network (LAN)
A group of computers, usually within a fairly limited space, that are physically connected to one another.

Lynx
A character-based Web browsing tool developed at the University of Kansas.

Mail Reflector
An eMail address that forwards mail to many other locations, such as participants in a particular discussion group.

Mail Server
A computer on a network that acts as a storage place for eMail messages. Similar to a file server, a mail server stores messages that have been sent by one user until the intended recipient retrieves them.

MIME (Multipurpose Internet Mail Extensions)
A format that allows nontext media files to be attached to eMail messages, such as audio or graphic features.

Modem
A device that connects a computer to a communication link for data transmission.

Mosaic

A graphical user interface (browser) for the World Wide Web, developed at the University of Illinois, available free to the Internet community.

MPEG (Moving Pictures Expert Group)

An internationally recognized protocol for video compression. A viewing tool is needed to watch MPEG "desktop movies" on your computer.

MUD/MOO

MUD refers to "Multi-User Dungeon," a series of computer games based on the "Dungeons and Dragons" game. MUDs have been modified for use as educational and conferencing tools. MOO refers to Object-Oriented MUD.

Multimedia

Generally refers to different forms of data, such as text, audio or video, that may appear in a document.

NCSA

The National Center for Supercomputing Applications at the University of Illinois. Developers of Mosaic, NCSA Telnet, and a number of other freeware applications.

NCSA Telnet

An application that allows users to remotely log into hosts running the TELNET protocol.

NetScape

Client and server software available from **http://www.netscape.com/**.

Network

A collection of computers and peripherals that are able to communicate with each other via some set of network protocols.

NFS

The Network File System; a set of protocols that allows you to read, write or edit a file that sits on another computer in your network, using the same commands that you would use if the file existed locally, eliminating the need to "FTP" transfer the file to your machine to perform these tasks.

NIC (Network Information Center)

An organization that provides information about networks.

Node

A term used to describe a device that can access a network, such as a computer or printer.

NSFNET (National Science Foundation Network)

The National Science Foundation Network is one of the networks that comprise the Internet.

Packet

A bundle of data that travels across the Internet independently, usually in sizes of 1500 bytes or less.

Port

A port number delineates the particular Net application that is being used by a computer when it sends packets of information to another computer. A port is also a "jack" on the back of a computer that is used to connect a hardware accessory, such as a modem. The default port for a Web server is port 80.

Posting

A message sent to a UseNet newsgroup, or the act of sending the message.

PPP (Point-to-Point Protocol)

A direct connection between a computer and the Internet (bypassing a typical host connection) using a modem and telephone lines, requiring PPP software, TCP and an IP address. PPP connections are usually obtained from an Internet provider.

PRI

Primary Rate Interface is the ISDN telecommunications standard capacity. It has two definitions depending on where you live. In the U.S., Canada, and Japan it is equivalent to 23 B Channels plus one D channel (23B+D, 1.544 Mbps capacity); in Europe it is equivalent to 31 B Channels plus one D channel (31B+D, 2.048 Mbps capacity).

Protocol

A set of rules which defines the way in which computers will communicate with each other by providing set patterns and formats for data transfer. Use of standard protocols allows different kinds of computers and software programs to exchange information.

Protocol Layers

The different layers of a protocol refer to the different steps the networking software must take to accomplish the variety of tasks required for successful data transmission.

Protocol Stack

Related layers of protocol software that function together to implement a particular communications process, such as AppleTalk.

Proxy Server

An internet server that allows one to indirectly access systems that have security "firewalls" prohibiting direct Internet access.

QuickTime
An Apple Computer video standard that runs as an extension file in the system folder. You need an additional viewing application to watch QuickTime "movies" on your screen.

RFC (Request for Comments)
Published documents describing the Internet's accepted and proposed standards and norms.

Router
Software or hardware that is used to join separate networks into larger internetworks. It can also be used to transfer information (packets) between two networks operating under the same protocols, but which may be mechanically different.

RTFM
A colorful abbreviation commonly used in eMail meaning "read the f%#@ing manual."

Security Firewall
A method of preventing direct Internet access to computers on a network by filtering or blocking certain network protocols or addresses. It is used to maintain security and privacy. *See* Proxy Server.

Server
A computer that provides a variety of services, such as text libraries, file transfer, or eMail, to client computers.

Service Provider
See Internet Service Provider.

Session
A related group of communications transactions between different nodes on a network.

SGML (Standard Generalized Markup Language)
A document formatting protocol utilizing codes to define the parts of a document.

Shell
On a UNIX system, software that accepts and processes command lines from your terminal. UNIX has multiple shells available, each with slightly different command formats and facilities.

Signature
A file that some people place at the bottom of an eMail message or UseNet posting as a personal identification. They usually contain the sender's name and eMail address, and often include quotations, simple drawings, or other information.

SLIP (Serial Line Internet Protocol)
A direct connection between a computer and the Internet (as an alternative to a typical host connection) using a modem and telephone lines, requiring SLIP software, TCP and IP address. SLIP connections are usually obtained from an Internet provider.

SMTP (Simple Mail Transfer Protocol)
The eMail protocol designated for use in TCP/IP networks.

SNMP (Simple Network Management Protocol)
The TCP/IP network protocol for managing the various devices on a network.

Socket
A particular software process operating as a communications endpoint within a network device. Sockets are permanently assigned to the software process that they have been designated to service.

Socket Number
The number that identifies which socket within a node is assigned to carry out a particular software task.

SQL (Structured Query Language)
A data manipulation protocol standardized by ANSI, commonly used in relational databases.

Switched Access
A temporary network connection that is initiated when needed and sub-sequently discarded, such as a SLIP or PPP connection.

Synchronous Communication
A process of data transmission in which both the sender and receiver synchronize their clocks each time that a packet of data is exchanged.

Tags
The formatting codes in an HTML document that instruct the browsing software how to display the document's text, graphics or sounds.

TCP/IP (Transmission Control Protocol/Internet Protocol)
Two basic and important Internet protocols. TCP allows for the reliable transmission of packets of data. IP allows data to travel across different systems.

Telnet
An application that allows a computer to log into another system via the Telnet protocol. *See* NCSA Telnet.

Terminal Emulation
A popular network application in which a computer runs software that makes it appear to be a terminal across the network, allowing it to "speak the language" of a mainframe with which it might not otherwise be able to exchange data.

TIFF (Tagged Image File Format)
A graphic file format developed by Aldus and Microsoft that is commonly used as an image transfer protocol on computer networks.

Time Out
An interruption in the connection between two computers transversing a communications link.

UNIX
An operating system intimate to functions that occur on the Internet.

URL (Uniform Resource Locator)
A system of address identification for all materials on the World Wide Web, including the method of access and host computer to be contacted.

UseNet
A loosely structured, informal group that exchanges messages or "news" about a particular subject, usually over the Internet.

UUCP (UNIX-to-UNIX copy)
A protocol by which files are transported between UNIX systems.

Viewer
A program launched by a Web browser when it encounters a file that it can't translate or display.

W3O
An organization overseeing the future development of the World Wide Web, under the auspices of CERN and the Massachusetts Institute of Technology.

WAIS (Wide Area Information Service)
A service that helps one locate libraries and databases across the Internet.

WAIS Gateway

Networks that are not able to speak directly to WAIS use a WAIS gateway to translate the data into a compatible format.

WAN (Wide Area Network)

A system of networked computers that communicate over a large geographic area.

Web Browser

Software that allows a user to access and view HTML documents, such as Mosaic, Lynx, WinWeb, or Netscape.

WebMaster

The administrator of a World Wide Web site.

Web Node

Another term for a Web site or Web server.

Web Page

An HTML document that one accesses via the Web.

Webspace

A term used to describe the "space" on the World Wide Web.

Web Spider

A program that shows a map of the links that one has crossed over while browsing the Web.

Web Walking (Web surfing)

The act of traversing sites and documents on the World Wide Web via a Web browsing tool.

Workstation

A computer on a network.

World Wide Web
A method of locating and utilizing Internet resources via a graphical user interface (browser) and hyperlinks.

XBM
XBM files are XWindow system bitmaps.

Zines
See E-zines.

Appendix B

INTERNET PROVIDERS

We combed the Net and thumbed through back issues of Net magazines to come up with a comprehensive and up-to-date list of Internet providers for you. And basically, we give up. We've reproduced the best list we found, the one from Paul Celestin, on the next pages.

But better than any printed list are two excellent Web pages: The TAG Online Mall and Paul Celestin's comprehensive list of Internet providers (the Web page is guaranteed to be more up to date than the pages that follow).

Check out:

http://www.teleport.com/~cci/directories/pocia/pocia.html

and

http://www.tagsys.com/

We promised our friends at TAG we'd put a plug in for them, so that's not the exact address of the page with the list. That URL will force you to start at the TAG Home Page, which will make you to check out a nifty example of a Web mall on your way to the list, which is easy to find from the home page. By the way, this site has a great searchable database.

And now, here's Paul Celestin's list as of February 1995, reprinted here with his kind permission.

Providers of Commercial Internet Access (POCIA) Directory

Updated 7 February 1995. Copyright 1994–1995 by Celestin Company, Inc. All rights reserved worldwide. The information in this directory is provided as-is and without any expressed or implied warranties, including, without limitation, the implied warranties of merchantability and fitness for a particular purpose. You may use the information in this directory for non-commercial purposes only. Contact us if you wish to use the directory for a commercial purpose.

All of the information in this directory was supplied to Celestin Company directly by the service providers and is subject to change without notice.

This directory is brought to you as a public service. Celestin Company does not receive any compensation from the providers listed here. Since Internet service providers come and go, and frequently change their offers, we strongly urge you to contact them for additional information and/or restrictions.

The latest version of this document is available at the following location:

ftp://ftp.teleport.com/vendors/cci/pocia/pocia.txt

You may also retrieve the latest copy (as well as additional information on Celestin Company and its products) using eMail. For information on how this works, send a blank message to:

cci@olympus.net

If you have Web access, try

http://www.teleport.com/~cci/

for the hypertext version of this list, which includes addresses, telephone numbers, fax numbers, eMail addresses, and pricing.

U.S. and Canada Service Providers

A listing of Internet service providers in the U.S. and Canada, sorted by area code. Fields are service provider name and service types offered, phone number, and eMail address for more information.

Free Service Providers

Service Provider	Phone	eMail
Cyberspace (shell,slip,ppp)	modem -> 515 945 7000	info@cyberspace.com
Free.org (shell,slip,ppp)	modem -> 715 743 1600	info@free.org
Free.I.Net (must dial via AT&T)	modem -> 801 471 2266	info@free.i.net
SLIPNET (shell,slip,ppp)	modem -> 217 792 2777	info@slip.net

Nationwide Service Providers

Service Provider	Phone	eMail
ANS	703 758 7700	info@ans.net
Global Connect, Inc.	804 229 4484	info@gc.net
Informed Access Technologies Holonet	510 704 0160	info@holonet.com
NETCOM On-Line Communications Services	408 554 8649	info@netcom.com
Network 99, Inc.	800 NET 99IP	net99@cluster.mcs.net
Performance Systems International	800 827 7482	all-info@psi.com

Toll-Free Service Providers

Service Provider	Phone	eMail
American Information Systems, Inc.	708 413 8400	info@ais.net
Association for Computing Machinery	817 776 6876	account-info@acm.org
CICNet, Inc.	313 998 6103	info@cic.net
Colorado SuperNet, Inc.	303 296 8202	info@csn.org
DataBank, Inc.	913 842 6699	info@databank.com
Global Connect, Inc.	804 229 4484	info@gc.net
Internet Express	719 592 1240	info@usa.net
Msen, Inc.	313 998 4562	info@msen.com
NeoSoft, Inc.	713 684 5969	info@neosoft.com
New Mexico Technet, Inc.	505 345 6555	granoff@technet.nm.org
Pacific Rim Network, Inc.	360 650 0442	info@pacificrim.net
Prometheus Information Network Group Inc.	404 399 1670	info@ping.com
Rocky Mountain Internet	800 900 7644	info@rmii.com

Regional Service Providers (by Area Code)

Area Code 201

Service Provider	Phone	eMail
Carroll-Net	201 488 1332	info@carroll.com
The Connection	201 435 4414	info@cnct.com

Service Provider	Phone	eMail
Digital Express Group	301 220 2020	info@digex.net
INTAC Access Corporation	800 504 6822	info@intac.com
InterCom Online	212 714 7183	info@intercom.com
Internet Online Services	x226 -> 201 928 1000	help@ios.com
Mordor International BBS	201 433 4222	ritz@mordor.com
NETCOM On-Line Communications Services	408 554 8649	info@netcom.com
New York Net	718 776 6811	sales@new-york.net
NIC - Neighborhood Internet Connection	201 934 1445	info@nic.com

Area Code 202

Service Provider	Phone	eMail
CAPCON Library Network	202 331 5771	info@capcon.net
Charm.Net	410 558 3900	info@charm.net
Digital Express Group	301 220 2020	info@digex.net
Genuine Computing Resources	703 878 4680	info@gcr.com
Quantum Networking Solutions, Inc.	805 538 2028	info@qnet.com
US Net, Incorporated	301 572 5926	info@us.net

Area Code 203

Service Provider	Phone	eMail
Connix: Connecticut Internet Exchange	203 349 7059	info@connix.com
Futuris Networks, Inc.	203 359 8868	info@futuris.net
I-2000 Inc.	516 867 6379	info@i-2000.com
Paradigm Communications, Inc.	203 250 7397	info@pcnet.com

Area Code 205

Service Provider	Phone	eMail
Community Internet Connect, Inc.	205 722 0199	info@cici.com
interQuest, Inc.	205 464 8280	info@iquest.com

Area Code 206

Service Provider	Phone	eMail
Eskimo North	206 367 7457	nanook@eskimo.com
NETCOM On-Line Communications Services	408 554 8649	info@netcom.com
NorthWest CommLink	206 336 0103	info@nwcl.net
Northwest Nexus, Inc.	206 455 3505	info@nwnexus.wa.com
Pacifier Computers	206 254 3886	account@pacifier.com
Seanet Online Services	206 343 7828	info@seanet.com
SenseMedia	408 335 9400	sm@picosof.com

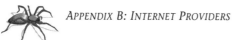

Service Provider	Phone	eMail
Skagit On-Line Services	206 755 0190	info@sos.net
Structured Network Systems, Inc.	503 656 3530	info@structured.net
Teleport, Inc.	503 223 4245	info@teleport.com
Transport Logic	503 243 1940	sales@transport.com

Area Code 207

Service Provider	Phone	eMail
Agate Internet Services	207 947 8248	ais@agate.net

Area Code 208

Service Provider	Phone	eMail
Minnesota Regional Network	612 342 2570	info@mr.net
NICOH Net	208 233 5802	info@nicoh.com
Primenet	602 870 1010	info@primenet.com
Transport Logic	503 243 1940	sales@transport.com

Area Code 209

Service Provider	Phone	eMail
Cybergate Information Services	209 486 4283	cis@cybergate.com
West Coast Online	707 586 3060	info@calon.com

Area Code 212

Service Provider	Phone	eMail
Alternet (UUNET Technologies, Inc.)	703 204 8000	info@alter.net
Blythe Systems	212 226 7171	infodesk@blythe.org
Creative Data Consultants (SILLY.COM)	718 229 0489	info@silly.com
Digital Express Group	301 220 2020	info@digex.net
Echo Communications Group	212 255 3839	info@echonyc.com
escape.com—Kazan Corp	212 888 8780	info@escape.com
Ingress Communications Inc.	212 679 2838	info@ingress.com
INTAC Access Corporation	800 504 6822	info@intac.com
InterCom Online	212 714 7183	info@intercom.com
Internet Online Services	x226 -> 201 928 1000	help@ios.com
Interport Communications Corp.	212 989 1128	info@interport.net
Mordor International BBS	201 433 4222	ritz@mordor.com
NETCOM On-Line Communications Services	408 554 8649	info@netcom.com
New York Net	718 776 6811	sales@new-york.net
Phantom Access Technologies, Inc.	212 989 2418	bruce@phantom.com
The Pipeline Network	212 267 2626	info-info@pipeline.com

Area Code 213

Service Provider	Phone	eMail
Abode Computer Service	818 287 5115	eric@abode.ttank.com
Delta Internet Services	714 778 0370	info@deltanet.com
DigiLink Network Services	310 542 7421	info@digilink.net
DirectNet	213 383 3144	info@directnet.com
EarthLink Network, Inc.	213 644 9500	info@earthlink.net
Electriciti	619 338 9000	info@powergrid.electriciti.com
KAIWAN Corporation	714 638 2139	info@kaiwan.com
Primenet	602 870 1010	info@primenet.com
ViaNet Communications	415 903 2242	info@via.net

Area Code 214

Service Provider	Phone	eMail
Alternet (UUNET Technologies, Inc.)	703 204 8000	info@alter.net
DFW Internet Services, Inc.	817 332 5116	info@dfw.net
NETCOM On-Line Communications Services	408 554 8649	info@netcom.com
Texas Metronet, Inc.	214 705 2900	info@metronet.com

Area Code 215

Service Provider	Phone	eMail
FishNet	610 337 9994	info@pond.com
Microserve Information Systems	717 779 4430	info@microserve.com
Oasis Telecommunications, Inc.	610 439 8560	staff@oasis.ot.com
YOU TOOLS Corporation	610 954 5910	info@youtools.com

Area Code 216

Service Provider	Phone	eMail
APK Public Access UNI* Site	216 481 9436	info@wariat.org
Branch Information Services	313 741 4442	branch-info@branch.com
Exchange Network Services, Inc.	216 261 4593	info@en.com
OARnet (corporate clients only)	614 728 8100	info@oar.net

Area Code 218

Service Provider	Phone	eMail
Red River Net	701 232 2227	info@rrnet.com

Area Code 301

Service Provider	Phone	eMail
Charm.Net	410 558 3900	info@charm.net
Clark Internet Services, Inc. Clark-Net	410 995 0691	info@clark.net
Digital Express Group	301 220 2020	info@digex.net
Genuine Computing Resources	703 878 4680	info@gcr.com
Quantum Networking Solutions, Inc.	805 538 2028	info@qnet.com
SURAnet	301 982 4600	marketing@sura.net
US Net, Incorporated	301 572 5926	info@us.net

Area Code 302

Service Provider	Phone	eMail
SSNet, Inc.	302 378 1386	info@ssnet.com

Area Code 303

Service Provider	Phone	eMail
Colorado SuperNet, Inc.	303 296 8202	info@csn.org
Internet Express	719 592 1240	info@usa.net
NETCOM On-Line Communications Services	408 554 8649	info@netcom.com
New Mexico Technet, Inc.	505 345 6555	granoff@technet.nm.org
Rocky Mountain Internet	800 900 7644	info@rmii.com

Area Code 305

Service Provider	Phone	eMail
Acquired Knowledge Systems Inc.	305 525 2574	info@aksi.net
CyberGate, Inc.	305 428 4283	sales@gate.net
InteleCom Data Systems, Inc.	401 885 6855	info@ids.net
SatelNET Communications	305 434 8738	admin@satelnet.org

Area Code 310

Service Provider	Phone	eMail
Abode Computer Service	818 287 5115	eric@abode.ttank.com
Cloverleaf Communications	714 895 3075	sales@cloverleaf.com
Delta Internet Services	714 778 0370	info@deltanet.com
DigiLink Network Services	310 542 7421	info@digilink.net
EarthLink Network, Inc.	213 644 9500	info@earthlink.net
KAIWAN Corporation	714 638 2139	info@kaiwan.com
Lightside, Inc.	818 858 9261	info@lightside.com
NETCOM On-Line Communications Services	408 554 8649	info@netcom.com
ViaNet Communications	415 903 2242	info@via.net

Area Code 312

Service Provider	Phone	eMail
American Information Systems, Inc.	708 413 8400	info@ais.net
CICNet, Inc.	313 998 6103	info@cic.net
InterAccess Co.	800 967 1580	info@interaccess.com
MCSNet	312 248 8649	info@mcs.net
NETCOM On-Line Communications Services	408 554 8649	info@netcom.com
Open Business Systems, Inc.	708 250 0260	info@obs.net
Ripco Communications, Inc.	312 477 6210	info@ripco.com
Tezcatlipoca, Inc.	312 850 0181	info@tezcat.com
WorldWide Access	708 367 1870	info@wwa.com

Area Code 313

Service Provider	Phone	eMail
Branch Information Services	313 741 4442	branch-info@branch.com
CICNet, Inc.	313 998 6103	info@cic.net
ICNET / Innovative Concepts	313 998 0090	info@ic.net
Msen, Inc.	313 998 4562	info@msen.com

Area Code 314

Service Provider	Phone	eMail
NeoSoft, Inc.	713 684 5969	info@neosoft.com
ThoughtPort, Inc.	314 474 6870	info@thoughtport.com

Area Code 315

Service Provider	Phone	eMail
ServiceTech Inc. Cyber-Link	716 546 6908	dam@cyber1.servtech.com

Area Code 316

Service Provider	Phone	eMail
SouthWind Internet Access, Inc.	316 263 7963	info@southwind.net

Area Code 317

Service Provider	Phone	eMail
Branch Information Services	313 741 4442	branch-info@branch.com
IQuest Network Services	317 259 5050	info@iquest.net

Area Code 360

Service Provider	Phone	eMail
Pacific Rim Network, Inc.	360 650 0442	info@pacificrim.net
Townsend Communications, Inc.	360 385 0464	info@olympus.net
Whidbey Connections, Inc.	360 678 1070	info@whidbey.net

Area Code 401

Service Provider	Phone	eMail
InteleCom Data Systems, Inc.	401 885 6855	info@ids.net

Area Code 402

Service Provider	Phone	eMail
Internet Nebraska	402 434 8680	info@inetnebr.com

Area Code 403

Service Provider	Phone	eMail
Debug Computer Services	403 248 5798	root@debug.cuc.ab.ca
UUNET Canada, Inc.	416 368 6621	info@uunet.ca

Area Code 404

Service Provider	Phone	eMail
Internet Atlanta	404 410 9000	info@atlanta.com
MindSpring	404 888 0725	info@mindspring.com
NETCOM On-Line Communications Services	408 554 8649	info@netcom.com
Prometheus Information Network Group Inc.	404 399 1670	info@ping.com

Area Code 405

Service Provider	Phone	eMail
Internet Oklahoma	405 721 1580	info@ionet.net
Questar Network Services	405 848 3228	info@qns.net

Area Code 406

Service Provider	Phone	eMail
Montana Online	406 721 4952	info@montana.com

Area Code 407

Service Provider	Phone	eMail
CyberGate, Inc.	305 428 4283	sales@gate.net
Florida Online	407 635 8888	info@digital.net

Service Provider	Phone	eMail
InteleCom Data Systems, Inc.	401 885 6855	info@ids.net
InternetU	407 952 8487	info@iu.net
MagicNet, Inc.	407 657 2202	info@magicnet.net

Area Code 408

Service Provider	Phone	eMail
Aimnet Information Services	408 257 0900	info@aimnet.com
Alternet (UUNET Technologies, Inc.)	703 204 8000	info@alter.net
BTR Communications Company	415 966 1429	support@btr.com
Direct Net Access Incorporated	510 649 6110	support@dnai.com
The Duck Pond Public Unix	modem -> 408 249 9630	postmaster@kfu.com
Electriciti	619 338 9000	info@powergrid.electriciti.com
Infoserv Connections	408 335 5600	root@infoserv.com
InterNex Information Services, Inc.	415 473 3060	info@internex.net
ISP Networks	408 653 0100	info@isp.net
NETCOM On-Line Communications Services	408 554 8649	info@netcom.com
Scruz-Net	408 457 5050	info@scruz.net
SenseMedia	408 335 9400	sm@picosof.com
South Valley Internet	408 683 4533	info@garlic.com
West Coast Online	707 586 3060	info@calon.com

Service Provider	Phone	eMail
zNET	619 755 7772	info@znet.com
Zocalo Engineering	510 540 8000	info@zocalo.net

Area Code 409

Service Provider	Phone	eMail
Internet Connect Services, Inc.	512 572 9987	info@icsi.net

Area Code 410

Service Provider	Phone	eMail
CAPCON Library Network	202 331 5771	info@capcon.net
Charm.Net	410 558 3900	info@charm.net
Clark Internet Services, Inc. Clark-Net	410 995 0691	info@clark.net
Digital Express Group	301 220 2020	info@digex.net
US Net, Incorporated	301 572 5926	info@us.net

Area Code 412

Service Provider	Phone	eMail
Telerama Public Access Internet	412 481 3505	info@telerama.lm.com

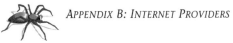

Area Code 413

Service Provider	Phone	eMail
Mallard Electronics, Inc.	413 732 0214	gheacock@map.com
ShaysNet.COM	413 772 3774	staff@shaysnet.com

Area Code 414

Service Provider	Phone	eMail
Exec-PC, Inc.	414 789 4200	info@execpc.com
FullFeed Communications	608 246 4239	info@fullfeed.com
MIX Communications	414 351 1868	info@mixcom.com

Area Code 415

Service Provider	Phone	eMail
Aimnet Information Services	408 257 0900	info@aimnet.com
Alternet (UUNET Technologies, Inc.)	703 204 8000	info@alter.net
BTR Communications Company	415 966 1429	support@btr.com
Community ConneXion - NEXUS-Berkeley	510 549 1383	info@c2.org
Direct Net Access Incorporated	510 649 6110	support@dnai.com
InterNex Information Services, Inc.	415 473 3060	info@internex.net
LineX Communications	415 455 1650	info@linex.com
NETCOM On-Line Communications Services	408 554 8649	info@netcom.com

Service Provider	Phone	eMail
QuakeNet	415 655 6607	info@quake.net
SLIPNET	415 281 3132	info@slip.net
ViaNet Communications	415 903 2242	info@via.net
The WELL	415 332 4335	info@well.com
West Coast Online	707 586 3060	info@calon.com
zNET	619 755 7772	info@znet.com
Zocalo Engineering	510 540 8000	info@zocalo.net

Area Code 416

Service Provider	Phone	eMail
HookUp Communications	905 847 8000	info@hookup.net
InterLog Internet Services	416 975 2655	internet@interlog.com
UUNET Canada, Inc.	416 368 6621	info@uunet.ca

Area Code 418

Service Provider	Phone	eMail
UUNET Canada, Inc.	416 368 6621	info@uunet.ca

Area Code 419

Service Provider	Phone	eMail
Branch Information Services	313 741 4442	branch-info@branch.com
OARnet (corporate clients only)	614 728 8100	info@oar.net

Area Code 501

Service Provider	Phone	eMail
Cloverleaf Technologies	903 832 1367	helpdesk@clo-ver.cleaf.com
Sibylline, Inc.	501 521 4660	info@sibylline.com

Area Code 502

Service Provider	Phone	eMail
IgLou Internet Services	800 436 4456	info@iglou.com

Area Code 503

Service Provider	Phone	eMail
Alternet (UUNET Technologies, Inc.)	703 204 8000	info@alter.net
Data Research Group, Inc.	503 465 3282	info@ordata.com
Europa	503 222 9508	info@europa.com
Hevanet Communications	503 228 3520	info@hevanet.com

Service Provider	Phone	eMail
NETCOM On-Line Communications Services	408 554 8649	info@netcom.com
Open Door Networks, Inc.	503 488 4127	info@opendoor.com
RainDrop Laboraties	503 293 1772	info@agora.rdrop.com
Structured Network Systems, Inc.	503 656 3530	info@structured.net
Teleport, Inc.	503 223 4245	info@teleport.com
Transport Logic	503 243 1940	sales@transport.com

Area Code 504

Service Provider	Phone	eMail
Communique Inc.	504 527 6200	info@communique.net
NeoSoft, Inc.	713 684 5969	info@neosoft.com

Area Code 505

Service Provider	Phone	eMail
Computer Systems Consulting	505 984 0085	info@spy.org
Internet Express	719 592 1240	info@usa.net
New Mexico Technet, Inc.	505 345 6555	granoff@technet.nm.org
Southwest Cyberport	505 271 0009	info@swcp.com
ZyNet SouthWest	505 343 8846	zycor@zynet.com

Area Code 506

Service Provider	Phone	eMail
Agate Internet Services	207 947 8248	ais@agate.net

Area Code 507

Service Provider	Phone	eMail
Internet Connections, Inc.	507 625 7320	info@ic.mankato.mn.us
Millennium Communications, Inc.	612 338 5509	info@millcomm.com
Minnesota Regional Network	612 342 2570	info@mr.net

Area Code 508

Service Provider	Phone	eMail
The Destek Group, Inc.	603 635 3857	inquire@destek.net
FOURnet Information Network	508 291 2900	info@four.net
The Internet Access Company (TIAC)	617 276 7200	info@tiac.net
intuitive information, inc.	508 341 1100	info@iii.net
North Shore Access	617 593 3110	info@shore.net
SCHUNIX	508 853 0258	schu@schunix.com
StarNet	508 922 8238	info@venus.star.net
UltraNet Communications, Inc.	508 229 8400	info@ultra.net.com
The World	617 739 0202	info@world.std.com

Service Provider	Phone	eMail
Wrentham Internet Services	508 384 1404	info@riva.com
Wilder Systems, Inc.	617 933 8810	info@id.wing.net

Area Code 509

Service Provider	Phone	eMail
Internet On-Ramp	509 927 7267	info@on-ramp.ior.com
Transport Logic	503 243 1940	sales@transport.com

Area Code 510

Service Provider	Phone	eMail
Alternet (UUNET Technologies, Inc.)	703 204 8000	info@alter.net
BTR Communications Company	415 966 1429	support@btr.com
Community ConneXion—NEXUS-Berkeley	510 549 1383	info@c2.org
Direct Net Access Incorporated	510 649 6110	support@dnai.com
InterNex Information Services, Inc.	415 473 3060	info@internex.net
LanMinds, Inc.	510 843 6389	info@lanminds.com
LineX Communications	415 455 1650	info@linex.com
NETCOM On-Line Communications Services	408 554 8649	info@netcom.com
SLIPNET	415 281 3132	info@slip.net
West Coast Online	707 586 3060	info@calon.com
Zocalo Engineering	510 540 8000	info@zocalo.net

Area Code 512

Service Provider	Phone	eMail
@sig.net	512 306 0700	sales@aus.sig.net
Internet Connect Services, Inc.	512 572 9987	info@icsi.net
NETCOM On-Line Communications Services	408 554 8649	info@netcom.com
Real/Time Communications	512 451 0046	info@realtime.net
Zilker Internet Park, Inc.	512 206 3850	info@zilker.net

Area Code 513

Service Provider	Phone	eMail
The Dayton Network Access Company	513 237 6868	info@dnaco.net
IgLou Internet Services	800 436 4456	info@iglou.com
Internet Access Cincinnati	513 887 8877	info@iac.net
Local Internet Gateway Co.	510 503 9227	sdw@lig.net
OARnet (corporate clients only)	614 728 8100	info@oar.net

Area Code 514

Service Provider	Phone	eMail
Communication Accessibles Montreal	514 288 2581	info@cam.org
Communications Inter-Acces	514 367 0002	info@interax.net
UUNET Canada, Inc.	416 368 6621	info@uunet.ca

Area Code 516

Service Provider	Phone	eMail
Creative Data Consultants (SILLY.COM)	718 229 0489	info@silly.com
Echo Communications Group	212 255 3839	info@echonyc.com
I-2000 Inc.	516 867 6379	info@i-2000.com
LI Net, Inc.	516 476 1168	info@li.net
Long Island Information, Inc.	516 294 0124	info@liii.com
Network Internet Services	516 543 0234	info@netusa.net
Phantom Access Technologies, Inc.	212 989 2418	bruce@phantom.com
The Pipeline Network	212 267 2626	info-info@pipeline.com

Area Code 517

Service Provider	Phone	eMail
Branch Information Services	313 741 4442	branch-info@branch.com
Msen, Inc.	313 998 4562	info@msen.com

Area Code 518

Service Provider	Phone	eMail
wizvax communications	518 271 0049	info@wizvax.com

Area Code 519

Service Provider	Phone	eMail
HookUp Communications	905 847 8000	info@hookup.net
MGL Systems Computer Technologies Inc.	519 651 2713	info@mgl.ca
UUNET Canada, Inc.	416 368 6621	info@uunet.ca

Area Code 520

Service Provider	Phone	eMail
Opus One	602 324 0494	sales@opus1.com
RTD Systems & Networking, Inc.	602 318 0696	info@rtd.com

Area Code 602

Service Provider	Phone	eMail
Crossroads Communications	602 813 9040	crossroads@xroads.com
Internet Direct, Inc.	602 274 0100	info@indirect.com
Internet Express	719 592 1240	info@usa.net
NETCOM On-Line Communications Services	408 554 8649	info@netcom.com
New Mexico Technet, Inc.	505 345 6555	granoff@technet.nm.org
Opus One	602 324 0494	sales@opus1.com
Primenet	602 870 1010	info@primenet.com
RTD Systems & Networking, Inc.	602 318 0696	info@rtd.com

Area Code 603

Service Provider	Phone	eMail
Agate Internet Services	207 947 8248	ais@agate.net
The Destek Group, Inc.	603 635 3857	inquire@destek.net
MV Communications, Inc.	603 429 2223	info@mv.mv.com
NETIS Public Access Internet	603 437 1811	epoole@leotech.mv.com

Area Code 604

Service Provider	Phone	eMail
AMT Solutions Group, Inc. Island Net	604 727 6030	info@islandnet.com
Mind Link!	604 534 5663	info@mindlink.bc.ca
Okanagan Internet Junction	604 549 1036	info@junction.net
Sunshine Net, Inc.	604 886 4120	admin@sunshine.net
UUNET Canada, Inc.	416 368 6621	info@uunet.ca

Area Code 606

Service Provider	Phone	eMail
IgLou Internet Services	800 436 4456	info@iglou.com
Internet Access Cincinnati	513 887 8877	info@iac.net

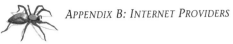

Area Code 608

Service Provider	Phone	eMail
FullFeed Communications	608 246 4239	info@fullfeed.com

Area Code 609

Service Provider	Phone	eMail
Digital Express Group	301 220 2020	info@digex.net
New Jersey Computer Connection	609 896 2799	info@pluto.njcc.com

Area Code 610

Service Provider	Phone	eMail
FishNet	610 337 9994	info@pond.com
Microserve Information Systems	717 779 4430	info@microserve.com
Oasis Telecommunications, Inc.	610 439 8560	staff@oasis.ot.com
SSNet, Inc.	302 378 1386	info@ssnet.com
YOU TOOLS Corporation	610 954 5910	info@youtools.com

Area Code 612

Service Provider	Phone	eMail
Millennium Communications, Inc.	612 338 5509	info@millcomm.com

Service Provider	Phone	eMail
Minnesota Regional Network	612 342 2570	info@mr.net
StarNet Communications, Inc.	612 941 9177	info@winternet.com

Area Code 613

Service Provider	Phone	eMail
Information Gateway Services	613 592 5619	info@igs.net
HookUp Communications	905 847 8000	info@hookup.net
o://info.web	613 225 3354	kevin@magi.com
UUNET Canada, Inc.	416 368 6621	info@uunet.ca

Area Code 614

Service Provider	Phone	eMail
Branch Information Services	313 741 4442	branch-info@branch.com
Internet Access Cincinnati	513 887 8877	info@iac.net
OARnet (corporate clients only)	614 728 8100	info@oar.net

Area Code 615

Service Provider	Phone	eMail
ERC, Inc. / The Edge	615 455 9915	staff@edge.ercnet.com
GoldSword Systems	615 691 6498	info@goldsword.com

Service Provider	Phone	eMail
ISDN-Net Inc	615 377 7672	jdunlap@rex.isdn.net
Telalink Corporation	615 321 9100	sales@telalink.net

Area Code 616

Service Provider	Phone	eMail
Branch Information Services	313 741 4442	branch-info@branch.com
Msen, Inc.	313 998 4562	info@msen.com

Area Code 617

Service Provider	Phone	eMail
Alternet (UUNET Technologies, Inc.)	703 204 8000	info@alter.net
The Internet Access Company (TIAC)	617 276 7200	info@tiac.net
intuitive information, inc.	508 341 1100	info@iii.net
NETCOM On-Line Communications Services	408 554 8649	info@netcom.com
North Shore Access	617 593 3110	info@shore.net
UltraNet Communications, Inc.	508 229 8400	info@ultra.net.com
Wilder Systems, Inc.	617 933 8810	info@id.wing.net
The World	617 739 0202	info@world.std.com

Area Code 619

Service Provider	Phone	eMail
CTS Network Services (CTSNET)	619 637 3637	info@cts.com
The Cyberspace Station	619 634 2894	info@cyber.net
Electriciti	619 338 9000	info@powergrid.electric-iti.com
NETCOM On-Line Communications Services	408 554 8649	info@netcom.com

Area Code 701

Service Provider	Phone	eMail
Red River Net	701 232 2227	info@rrnet.com

Area Code 702

Service Provider	Phone	eMail
@wizard.com	702 871 4461	info@wizard.com
Great Basin Internet Services	702 829 2244	info@greatbasin.com
NETCOM On-Line Communications Services	408 554 8649	info@netcom.com
Sierra-Net	702 831 3353	giles@sierra.net

Area Code 703

Service Provider	Phone	eMail
Alternet (UUNET Technologies, Inc.)	703 204 8000	info@alter.net
CAPCON Library Network	202 331 5771	info@capcon.net
Charm.Net	410 558 3900	info@charm.net
Clark Internet Services, Inc. ClarkNet	410 995 0691	info@clark.net
DataBank, Inc.	913 842 6699	info@databank.com
Digital Express Group	301 220 2020	info@digex.net
Genuine Computing Resources	703 878 4680	info@gcr.com
NETCOM On-Line Communications Services	408 554 8649	info@netcom.com
Quantum Networking Solutions, Inc.	805 538 2028	info@qnet.com
US Net, Incorporated	301 572 5926	info@us.net

Area Code 704

Service Provider	Phone	eMail
SunBelt.Net	803 328 1500	info@sunbelt.net
Vnet Internet Access	704 334 3282	info@vnet.net

Area Code 705

Service Provider	Phone	eMail
Mindemoya Computing	705 523 0243	info@mcd.on.ca

Area Code 706

Service Provider	Phone	eMail
Internet Atlanta	404 410 9000	info@atlanta.com
MindSpring	404 888 0725	info@mindspring.com

Area Code 707

Service Provider	Phone	eMail
West Coast Online	707 586 3060	info@calon.com
Zocalo Engineering	510 540 8000	info@zocalo.net

Area Code 708

Service Provider	Phone	eMail
American Information Systems, Inc.	708 413 8400	info@ais.net
CICNet, Inc.	313 998 6103	info@cic.net
InterAccess Co.	800 967 1580	info@interaccess.com
MCSNet	312 248 8649	info@mcs.net
Open Business Systems, Inc.	708 250 0260	info@obs.net

Service Provider	Phone	eMail
Ripco Communications, Inc.	312 477 6210	info@ripco.com
Tezcatlipoca, Inc.	312 850 0181	info@tezcat.com
WorldWide Access	708 367 1870	info@wwa.com

Area Code 713

Service Provider	Phone	eMail
Alternet (UUNET Technologies, Inc.)	703 204 8000	info@alter.net
The Black Box	713 480 2684	info@blkbox.com
Internet Connect Services, Inc.	512 572 9987	info@icsi.net
NeoSoft, Inc.	713 684 5969	info@neosoft.com
USiS	713 682 1666	admin@usis.com

Area Code 714

Service Provider	Phone	eMail
Cloverleaf Communications	714 895 3075	sales@cloverleaf.com
Delta Internet Services	714 778 0370	info@deltanet.com
DigiLink Network Services	310 542 7421	info@digilink.net
EarthLink Network, Inc.	213 644 9500	info@earthlink.net
Electriciti	619 338 9000	info@powergrid.electric-iti.com
KAIWAN Corporation	714 638 2139	info@kaiwan.com

Service Provider	Phone	eMail
Lightside, Inc.	818 858 9261	info@lightside.com
NETCOM On-Line Communications Services	408 554 8649	info@netcom.com

Area Code 715

Service Provider	Phone	eMail
FullFeed Communications	608 246 4239	info@fullfeed.com

Area Code 716

Service Provider	Phone	eMail
E-Znet, Inc.	716 262 2485	
ServiceTech Inc. Cyber-Link	716 546 6908	dam@cyber1.servtech.com

Area Code 717

Service Provider	Phone	eMail
Microserve Information Systems	717 779 4430	info@microserve.com
Oasis Telecommunications, Inc.	610 439 8560	staff@oasis.ot.com
YOU TOOLS Corporation	610 954 5910	info@youtools.com

Area Code 718

Service Provider	Phone	eMail
Blythe Systems	212 226 7171	infodesk@blythe.org
Creative Data Consultants (SILLY.COM)	718 229 0489	info@silly.com
escape.com - Kazan Corp	212 888 8780	info@escape.com
I-2000 Inc.	516 867 6379	info@i-2000.com
Ingress Communications Inc.	212 679 2838	info@ingress.com
InterCom Online	212 714 7183	info@intercom.com
Interport Communications Corp.	212 989 1128	info@interport.net
Mordor International BBS	201 433 4222	ritz@mordor.com
Phantom Access Technologies, Inc.	212 989 2418	bruce@phantom.com
The Pipeline Network	212 267 2626	info-info@pipeline.com

Area Code 719

Service Provider	Phone	eMail
Colorado SuperNet, Inc.	303 296 8202	info@csn.org
Internet Express	719 592 1240	info@usa.net
Old Colorado City Communications	719 528 5849	thefox@oldcolo.com
Rocky Mountain Internet	800 900 7644	info@rmii.com

Area Code 801

Service Provider	Phone	eMail
Infonaut Communication Services	801 370 3068	info@infonaut.com
Internet Direct, Inc.	801 578 0300	info@indirect.com
XMission	801 539 0852	support@xmission.com

Area Code 803

Service Provider	Phone	eMail
Global Vision Inc.	803 241 0901	info@globalvision.net
SIMS, Inc.	803 762 4956	info@sims.net
SunBelt.Net	803 328 1500	info@sunbelt.net

Area Code 804

Service Provider	Phone	eMail
Widomaker Communication Service	804 253 7621	bloyall@widowmaker.com

Area Code 805

Service Provider	Phone	eMail
EarthLink Network, Inc.	213 644 9500	info@earthlink.net

Service Provider	Phone	eMail
Quantum Networking Solutions, Inc.	805 538 2028	info@qnet.com
Regional Alliance for Info Networking	805 967 7246	info@rain.org

Area Code 808

Service Provider	Phone	eMail
Hawaii OnLine	808 533 6981	support@aloha.net
LavaNet, Inc.	808 545 5282	info@lava.net
Pacific Information Exchange, Inc.	808 596 7494	info@pixi.com

Area Code 810

Service Provider	Phone	eMail
Branch Information Services	313 741 4442	branch-info@branch.com
ICNET / Innovative Concepts	313 998 0090	info@ic.net
Msen, Inc.	313 998 4562	info@msen.com
RustNet, Inc.	810 650 6812	info@rust.net

Area Code 812

Service Provider	Phone	eMail
IgLou Internet Services	800 436 4456	info@iglou.com

Area Code 813

Service Provider	Phone	eMail
CyberGate, Inc.	305 428 4283	sales@gate.net
Intelligence Network Online, Inc.	x22 -> 813 442 0114	info@intnet.net
PacketWorks, Inc.	813 446 8826	info@packet.net

Area Code 815

Service Provider	Phone	eMail
American Information Systems, Inc.	708 413 8400	info@ais.net
InterAccess Co.	800 967 1580	info@interaccess.com

Area Code 816

Service Provider	Phone	eMail
Primenet	602 870 1010	info@primenet.com

Area Code 817

Service Provider	Phone	eMail
Association for Computing Machinery	817 776 6876	account-info@acm.org
DFW Internet Services, Inc.	817 332 5116	info@dfw.net
Texas Metronet, Inc.	214 705 2900	info@metronet.com

Area Code 818

Service Provider	Phone	eMail
Abode Computer Service	818 287 5115	eric@abode.ttank.com
Delta Internet Services	714 778 0370	info@deltanet.com
DigiLink Network Services	310 542 7421	info@digilink.net
EarthLink Network, Inc.	213 644 9500	info@earthlink.net
KAIWAN Corporation	714 638 2139	info@kaiwan.com
Lightside, Inc.	818 858 9261	info@lightside.com
NETCOM On-Line Communications Services	408 554 8649	info@netcom.com
Primenet	602 870 1010	info@primenet.com
Regional Alliance for Info Networking	805 967 7246	info@rain.org
ViaNet Communications	415 903 2242	info@via.net

Area Code 819

Service Provider	Phone	eMail
o://info.web	613 225 3354	kevin@magi.com

Area Code 901

Service Provider	Phone	eMail
ISDN-Net Inc	615 377 7672	jdunlap@rex.isdn.net
Magibox Incorporated	901 757 7835	info@magibox.net

Area Code 903

Service Provider	Phone	eMail
Cloverleaf Technologies	903 832 1367	helpdesk@clo-ver.cleaf.com

Area Code 904

Service Provider	Phone	eMail
CyberGate, Inc.	305 428 4283	sales@gate.net
SymNet	904 385 1061	info@symnet.net

Area Code 905

Service Provider	Phone	eMail
HookUp Communications	905 847 8000	info@hookup.net
InterLog Internet Services	416 975 2655	internet@interlog.com
Vaxxine Computer Systems Inc.	905 562 3500	admin@vaxxine.com

Area Code 906

Service Provider	Phone	eMail
Branch Information Services	313 741 4442	branch-info@branch.com
Msen, Inc.	313 998 4562	info@msen.com

Area Code 908

Service Provider	Phone	eMail
Castle Network, Inc.	908 548 8881	request@castle.net
Digital Express Group	301 220 2020	info@digex.net
INTAC Access Corporation	800 504 6822	info@intac.com
Internet Online Services	x226 -> 201 928 1000	help@ios.com

Area Code 909

Service Provider	Phone	eMail
Delta Internet Services	714 778 0370	info@deltanet.com
KAIWAN Corporation	714 638 2139	info@kaiwan.com
Lightside, Inc.	818 858 9261	info@lightside.com

Area Code 910

Service Provider	Phone	eMail
Vnet Internet Access	704 334 3282	info@vnet.net

Area Code 912

Service Provider	Phone	eMail
Internet Atlanta	404 410 9000	info@atlanta.com

Area Code 913

Service Provider	Phone	eMail
DataBank, Inc.	913 842 6699	info@databank.com

Area Code 914

Service Provider	Phone	eMail
Cloud 9 Internet	914 682 0626	info@cloud9.net
Computer Solutions by Hawkinson	914 229 9853	info@mhv.net
Creative Data Consultants (SILLY.COM)	718 229 0489	info@silly.com
DataBank, Inc.	913 842 6699	info@databank.com
INTAC Access Corporation	800 504 6822	info@intac.com
I-2000 Inc.	516 867 6379	info@i-2000.com
InteleCom Data Systems, Inc.	401 885 6855	info@ids.net
Phantom Access Technologies, Inc.	212 989 2418	bruce@phantom.com
The Pipeline Network	212 267 2626	info-info@pipeline.com
TZ-Link	914 353 5443	drew@j51.com
WestNet Internet Services	914 967 7816	info@westnet.com

Area Code 915

Service Provider	Phone	eMail
Internet Access of El Paso	915 533 1525	rosteen@itsnet.com
New Mexico Technet, Inc.	505 345 6555	granoff@technet.nm.org

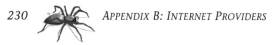

Area Code 916

Service Provider	Phone	eMail
Great Basin Internet Services	702 829 2244	info@greatbasin.com
NETCOM On-Line Communications Services	408 554 8649	info@netcom.com
Sierra-Net	702 831 3353	giles@sierra.net
West Coast Online	707 586 3060	info@calon.com
Zocalo Engineering	510 540 8000	info@zocalo.net

Area Code 918

Service Provider	Phone	eMail
Galaxy Star Systems	918 835 3655	info@galstar.com
Internet Oklahoma	918 583 1161	info@ionet.net

Area Code 919

Service Provider	Phone	eMail
NETCOM On-Line Communications Services	408 554 8649	info@netcom.com
Vnet Internet Access	704 334 3282	info@vnet.net

Foreign Service Providers

A listing of Internet service providers in countries other than the U.S. and Canada, sorted by country. Fields are country, service provider name, voice phone number, and email address for more information.

This list was prepared by:
    Celestin Company
    1152 Hastings Avenue
    Port Townsend, WA98368
    United States of America
    voice   360 385 3767
    fax   360 385 3586
    email   celestin@olympus.net

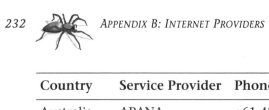

Country	Service Provider	Phone	eMail
Australia	APANA	+61 42 965015	wollongong@ apana.org.au
	Apanix Public Access	+61 8 373 5575	admin@apanix. apana.org.au
	arrakis.apana.org. au	+61 8 296 6200	greg@arrakis.apana.org.au
	AusNet Services Pty Ltd	+61 2 241 5888	sales@world.net
	Byron Public Access	+61 18 823 541	admin@byron.apana. org.au
	DIALix Services	+61 2 948 6995	justin@sydney.dialix. oz.au
	FidoNet Zone 3 Gateway	+61 3 793 2728	info@csource.pronet.com
	Hunter Network Association	+61 49 621783	mbrown@hna.com.au
	iiNet Technologies	+61 9 3071183	iinet@iinet.com.au
	Kralizec Dialup Unix System	+61 2 837 1397	nick@kralizec.zeta.org.au
	Informed Tech-nology	+61 9 245 2279	info@it.com.au
	The Message eXchange Pty Ltd	+61 2 550 5014	info@tmx.com.au
	Microplex Pty. Ltd.	+61 2 888 3685	info@mpx.com.au
	Pegasus Net-works Pty Ltd	+61 7 257 1111	fwhitmee@peg.apc.org
	PPIT Pty. Ltd. (059 051 320)	+61 3 747 9823	info@ppit.com.au
	Winthrop Technology	+61 9 380 3564	wthelp@yarrow. wt.uwa.edu.au

Country	Service Provider	Phone	eMail
Austria	EUnet EDV	+43 1 3174969	info@austria.eu.net
	Hochschueler-schaft...	+43 1 586 1868	sysop@link-atu.com-link.apc.org
	PING EDV	+43 1 3194336	info@ping.at
Bashkiria	UD JV 'DiasPro'	+7 3472 387454	iskander@diaspro.bash-kiria.su
Belarus	Open Contack, Ltd.	+7 172 272127	admin@brc.minsk.by
Belgium	EUnet Belgium NV	+32 16 236099	info@belgium.eu.net
	Infoboard Telematics SA	+32 2 475 25 31	ocaeymaex@infoboard.be
	INnet NV/SA	+32 14 319937	info@inbe.net
	KnoopPunt VZW	+32 9 2333 686	support@knooppunt.be
Bulgaria	EUnet Bulgaria	+359 52 259135	info@bulgaria.eu.net
Crimea	Crimea Communication Centre	+7 652 257214	sem@snail.crimea.ua
Denmark	DKnet / EUnet Denmark	+45 3917 9900	info@dknet.dk

Country	Service Provider	Phone	eMail
England	Compulink (CIX Ltd)	+44 181 390 8446	cixadmin@cix.compulink.co.uk
	CONNECT - PC User Group	+44 181 863 1191	info@ibmpcug.co.uk
	Demon Internet Services Ltd.	+44 81 349 0063	internet@demon.co.uk
	The Direct Connection	+44 81 313 0100	helpdesk@dircon.co.uk
	EUnet GB	+44 1227 266466	sales@britain.eu.net
	ExNet Systems Ltd.	+44 81 244 0077	info@exnet.com
	GreenNet	+44 71 713 1941	support@gn.apc.org
	Lunatech Research	+44 1734 791900	info@luna.co.uk
	Sound & Visions BBS	+44 1932 253131	info@span.com
	Specialix	+44 932 3522251	keith@specialix.co.uk
	WinNET (UK)	+44 181 863 1191	info@win-uk.ne
Finland	Clinet Ltd	+358 0 437 5209	clinet@clinet.fi
	EUnet Finland Ltd.	+358 0 400 2060	helpdesk@eunet.fi
France	French Data Network	+33 1 47975873	info@fdn.org
	OLEANE	+33 1 43283232	info-internet@oleane.net
Georgia	Mimosi Hard	+7 8832 232857	kisho@sanet.ge

Country	Service Provider	Phone	eMail
Germany	EUnet Germany GmbH	+49 231 972 2222	info@germany.eu.net
	Individual Network e.V.	+49 441 980 8556	in-info@individual.net
	INS Inter Networking Systems	+49 2305 356505	info@ins.net
	MUC.DE e.V.	+49 89 324 683 0	postmaster@muc.de
	PFM News & Mail Xlink POP	+49 171 331 0862	info@pfm.pfm-mainz.de
	SpaceNet GmbH	+49 89 324 683 0	info@space.net
Greece	Ariadne	+30 1 651 3392	dialup@leon.nrcps.ariadne-t.gr
	Foundation of Research	+30 81 221171	forthnet-pr@forthnet.gr
Hong Kong	Hong Kong SuperNet	+852 358 7924	trouble@hk.super.net
Iceland	SURIS / ISnet	+354 1 694747	isnet-info@isnet.is
Ireland	Ieunet Limited	+353 1 679 0832	info@ieunet.ie
	Ireland On-Line	+353 91 592727	info@iol.ie
Israel	Elronet	+972 313534	info@elron.net
	NetVision LTD.	+972 550330	info@netvision.net.il
Italy	ITnet S.p.A.	+39 10 6563324	info@it.net

Country	Service Provider	Phone	eMail
Japan	Global OnLine, Japan	+81 3 5330 9380	hahne@acm.org
	Internet Initiative Japan	+81 3 3580 3781	info@iij.ad.jp
	M.R.T., Inc.	+81 3 3255 8880	sysop@janis-tok.com
	People World Ltd.	+81 3 5661 4130	18005044@people.or.jp
	TWICS	+81 3 3351 5977	info@twics.com
	Typhoon Inc.	+81 3 3757 2118	info@typhoon.co.jp
Kazakhstan	Bogas Soft Laboratory Co.	+7 322 262 4990	pasha@sl.semsk.su
Kuwait	Gulfnet Kuwait	+965 242 6729	john@gulfa.ods. gulfnet.kw
Latvia	LvNet-Teleport	+371 2 551133	vit@riga.lv
	Versia Ltd.	+371 2 417000	postmaster@vernet.lv
Lisboa	Esoterica	716 2395	info@esoterica.com
Luxem-bourg	EUnet Luxemburg	+352 47 02 61 361	info@luxemburg.eu.net

Country	Service Provider	Phone	eMail
Netherlands	The Delft Connection	+31 15560079	info@void.tdcnet.nl
	Hobbynet	+31 365361683	henk@hgatenl.hobby.nl
	Internet Access Foundation	+31 5982 2720	mail-server@iafnl.iaf.nl
	NEST	+31 206265566	info@nest.nl
	NetLand	+31 206943664	info@netland.nl
	NLnet (EUnet)	+31 206639366	info@nl.net
	Psyline	+31 80445801	postmaster@psyline.nl
	Simplex Networking	+31 206932433	skelmir@simplex.nl
	Stichting XS4ALL	+31 206225222	helpdesk@xs4all.nl
New Zealand	Actrix Networks Limited	+64 4 389 6356	john@actrix.gen.nz
	Efficient Software Limited	+64 3 4738274	bart@dunedin.es.co.nz
Norway	Oslonett A/S	+47 22 46 10 99	oslonett@oslonett.no
Romania	EUnet Romania SRL	+40 1 312 6886	info@romania.eu.net
Russia	GlasNet	+7 95 262 7079	support@glas.apc.org
	InterCommunications Ltd.	+7 8632 620562	postmaster@ icomm.rnd.su
	N&K Company	+7 86622 72167	serge@nik.nalchik.su
	NEVAlink Ltd.	+7 812 592 3737	serg@arcom.spb.su
	Relcom CO	+7 95 194 25 40	postmaster@ussr.eu.net
	SvjazInform	+7 351 265 3600	pol@rich.chel.su
Slovakia	EUnet Slovakia	+42 7 725 306	info@slovakia.eu.net

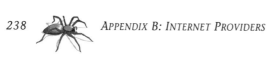

Country	Service Provider	Phone	eMail
Slovenia	NIL, System Integration	+386 61 1405 183	info@slovenia.eu.net
South Africa	Aztec	+27 21 419 2690	info@aztec.co.za
	Internet Africa	+27 0800 020003	info@iaccess.za
	The Internet Solution	+27 11 789 6071	info@is.co.za
Switzerland	SWITCH	+41 1 268 1515	postmaster@switch.ch
	XGP Switzerland	+41 61 8115635	service@xgp.spn.com
Tataretan	KAMAZ Incorporated	+7 8439 53 03 34	postmaster@ kamaz.kazan.su
Ukraine	ConCom, Ltd.	+7 0572 27 69 13	igor@ktts.kharkov.ua
	Electronni Visti	+7 44 2713457	info%elvisti.kiev.ua@ kiae.su
	PACO Links Int'l Ltd.	+7 48 2200057	info@vista.odessa.ua
	UkrCom-Kherson Ltd	+7 5522 64098	postmaster@ ukrcom.kherson.ua

Appendix C

NETSCAPE EXTENSIONS TO HTML

There's been much ado about the Netscape Communications "extensions" to HTML. It's interesting to watch the back and forth between a highly successful and innovative commercial concern and the traditional Internet standards people. It's not just with HTML that Netscape is pushing the envelope and creating a stir, either. The whole approach Netscape Communications is taking with its secure HTTP server and how it differs from the secure HTTP approach being adopted by others is another story unto itself.

We'll try to keep you up to date on the WebMaster WWW Server, but please realize it's a daunting task to try to keep up with it all.

At the time of this writing, Netscape had just released version 1.1b3 of its client and it was reported in many magazines and periodicals that three out of four Web surfers were using Netscape. Go to the Netscape Communications WWW server sometime for the whole story. You need to keep up with what they're up to. They are among the most innovative folks on the Net. If you want to get a handle on how they approach HTML and HTTP standards there's a great URL to check out at:

http://www.netscape.com/info/open-standards.html

Below are the extensions to HTML that Netscape first broke ground with around the time that HTML 2.0 was being set in stone. HTML 3.0 is in the works now, and, once again, Netscape is pushing the envelope with some innovative uses of HTML. The latest round of extensions and client features as of this writing includes the ability to do tables, backgrounds and animation. You can find the latest examples of those at:

http://home.netscape.com/home/demo/1.1b1/

Extensions to HTML

According to the folks at Netscape Communications, "extensions to HTML take the form of additional tags and attributes added to the HTML specification and are specifically designed not to break existing WWW browsers." The following info is right off their WWW server at **http://home.netscape.com/assist/net_sites/index** and is reprinted with the permision of Netscape Communications Corporation. Here is the page off their server with all the tags:

<ISINDEX>

To the ISINDEX element we have added the PROMPT tag. ISINDEX indicates that a document is a searchable index. PROMPT has been added so the document author can specify what message they want to appear before the text input field of the index. The default is of course that unfortunate message:

This is a searchable index. Enter search keywords:

<HR>

The HR element specifies that a horizontal rule of some sort (the default being a shaded engraved line) be drawn across the page. To this element we have added four new tags to allow the document author some ability to describe how the horizontal rule should look.

<HR SIZE=number>

The SIZE tag lets authors give an indication of how thick they wish the horizontal rule to be.

<HR WIDTH=number|percent>

The default horizontal rule is always as wide as the page. With the WIDTH tag, the author can specify an exact width in pixels, or a relative width measured in percent of document width.

<HR ALIGN=left|right|center>

Now that horizontal rules do not have to be the width of the page we need to allow the author to specify whether they should be pushed up against the left margin, the right margin, or centered in the page.

<HR NOSHADE>

Finally, for those times when you really want a solid bar, the NOSHADE tag lets you specify that you do not want any fancy shading of your horizontal rule.

<UL>

Your basic bulleted list has a default progression of bullet types that changes as you move through indented levels, from a solid disc, to a circle to a square. We have added a TYPE tag to the UL element so no matter what your indent level you can specify whether you want a TYPE=disc, TYPE=circle, or TYPE=square as your bullet.

<OL>

Your average ordered list counts 1, 2, 3, … etc. We have also added the TYPE tag to this element to allow authors to specify whether the want their list items marked with: capital letters (TYPE=A), small letters (TYPE=a), large roman numerals (TYPE=I), small roman numerals (TYPE=i), or the default numbers (TYPE=1).

For lists that wish to start at values other than 1 we have the new tag START. START is always specified in the default numbers, and will be converted based on TYPE before display. Thus START=5 would display either an 'E', 'e', 'V', 'v', or '5' based on the TYPE tag.

<LI>

To give even more flexibility to lists, we thought it would be nice if the author could change the list type, and for ordered lists the list count index as they progressed. To this end we added the TYPE tag to the LI element as well. It takes the same values as either UL or OL depending on the type of list you are in, and it changes the list type for that item, and all subsequent items. For ordered lists we have also added the VALUE element so you can change the count, for that list item and all subsequent.

<IMG>

The IMG tag is probably the most extended tag.

```
<IMG ALIGN=left|right|top|texttop|middle|absmiddle|
baseline|bottom|absbottom>
```

The additions to your ALIGN options need a lot of explanation. First, the values "left" and "right". Images with those alignments are an entirely new floating image type. An ALIGN=left image will float down and over to the left margin (into the next available space there), and subsequent text will wrap around the right-hand side of that image. Likewise for ALIGN=right the image aligns with the right margin, and the text wraps around the left.

The rest of the align options are my way of trying to correct for the horrible errors I made when first implementing the IMG tag, without destroying the look of existing documents. ALIGN=top does just what it always did, which is align itself with the top of the tallest item in the line. ALIGN=texttop does what many people thought top should do, which is align itself with the top of the tallest text in the line (this is usually but not always the same as ALIGN=top). ALIGN=middle does just what it always did, it aligns the baseline of the current line with the middle of the image. ALIGN=absmiddle does what middle should have done, which is align the middle of the current line with the middle of the image. ALIGN=baseline aligns the bottom of the image with the baseline of the current line. ALIGN=bottom does just what it always did (which is identical to ALIGN=baseline, but baseline is a better name). ALIGN=absbottom does what bottom should have done, which is align the bottom of the image with the bottom of the current line.

<IMG WIDTH=value HEIGHT=value>

The WIDTH and HEIGHT tags were added to IMG mainly to speed up display of the document. If the author specifies these, the viewer of their document will not have to wait for the image to be loaded over the network and its size calculated.

<IMG BORDER=value>

This lets the document author control the thickness of the border around an image displayed. Warning: setting BORDER=0 on images that are also part of anchors may confuse your users as they are used to a colored border indicating an image is an anchor.

<IMG VSPACE=value HSPACE=value>

For the floating images it is likely that the author does not want them pressing up against the text wrapped around the image. VSPACE controls the vertical space above and below the image, while HSPACE controls the horizontal space to the left and right of the image.

**
**

With the addition of floating images, we needed to expand the BR tag. Normal BR still just inserts a line break. We have added a CLEAR tag to BR, so CLEAR=left will break the line, and move vertically down until you have a clear left margin (no floating images). CLEAR=right does the same for the right margin, and CLEAR=all moves down until both margins are clear of images.

New Elements

<NOBR>

The NOBR element stands for NO BReak. This means all the text between the start and end of the NOBR elements cannot have line breaks inserted between them. While NOBR is essential for those odd character sequences you really don't want broken, please be careful; long text strings inside of NOBR elements can look rather odd.

<WBR>

The WBR element stands for Word BReak. This is for the very rare case when you have a NOBR section and you know exactly where you want it to break. Also, it's for any time you want to give the Netscape Navigator help by telling it where a word is allowed to be broken. The WBR element does not force a line break (BR does that) it simply lets the Netscape Navigator know where a line break is allowed to be inserted if needed.

<FONT SIZE=value>

Surprise! You can change the font size. Valid values range from 1–7. The default font size is 3. The value given to size can optionally have a '+' or '-' character in front of it to specify that it is relative to the document basefont. The default basefont is 3, and can be changed with the BASEFONT element.

<BASEFONT SIZE=value>

This changes the size of the BASEFONT that all relative font changes are based on. It defaults to 3, and has a valid range of 1–7.

<CENTER>

You aren't dreaming; yes, you can center your text. All lines of text between the begin and end of CENTER are centered between the current left and right margins. A new tag has been introduced rather than using the proposed <P Align="center"> because using <P Align="center"> breaks many existing browsers when the <P> tag is used as a container. The <P Align="center"> tag is also less general and does not support all cases where centering may be desired.

Behavioral Changes

Font attributes are now properly cumulative. Text inside something like <tt><font size=6>Text here</font></tt> will be italic fixed bold text of size 6.

The Netscape Navigator should now properly deal with the awful HTML comment sequence. This should be:

<!-- Comment here -->

These comments can include other elements, and thus be used to quickly comment out large chunks of markup.

Line breaking is a little more under control now. Unless specified with a formatting element, lines can only be broken where empty space occurs in the original document. This means any spaces, tabs, or new lines. You should never again have the sequence <A HREF=url>Anchor here</A>. broken between the highlighted anchor and the period.

New Entities

In addition to the usual & escaped entities:

® -> Registered Trademark -> ®

© -> Copyright -> ©

Tables as Implemented in Netscape 1.1

Netscape 1.1 and the Proposed HTML 3.0 Specification

As you can see in a few examples, it's been interesting trying to faithfully reproduce tables as described in the HTML 3.0 proposed specification in Netscape 1.1, because as fast as we implement something, the proposed spec changes. The only consolation is that, someday, the spec will become the standard and stop changing.

The Table Tags

<TABLE ...></TABLE>

This is the main wrapper for all the other table tags, and other table tags will be ignored if they aren't wrapped inside of a TABLE tag. By default, tables have no borders; borders will be added if the BORDER attribute is specified.

Right now TABLE has an implied linebreak both before and after it. We expect this to change so that you can eventually have as much control over placement of tables as you currently do over the placement of images — aligning them to various positions in a line of text, as well as shifting them to the left or right margins and wrapping text around them.

<TR ...></TR>

This stands for table row. The number of rows in a table is exactly specified by how many TR tags are contained within it, regardless of cells that may attempt to use the ROWSPAN attribute to span into non-specified rows. TR can have both the ALIGN and VALIGN attributes, which if specified become the default alignments for all cells in this row.

<TD ...></TD>

This stands for table data, and specifies a standard table data cell. Table data cells must only appear within table rows. Each row need not have the same number of cells specified, as short rows will be padded with blank cells on the right. A cell can contain any of the HTML tags normally present in the body of an HTML document. The default alignment of table data is ALIGN=left and VALIGN=middle. These alignments are overridden by any alignments specified in the containing TR tag, and those alignments in turn are overridden by any ALIGN or VALIGN attributes explicitly specified on this cell. By default, lines inside of table cells can be broken up to fit within the overall cell width. Specifying the NOWRAP attribute for a TD prevents linebreaking for that cell.

<TH ...></TH>

This stands for table header. Header cells are identical to data cells in all respects, with the exception that header cells are in a bold FONT, and have a default ALIGN=center.

<CAPTION ...></CAPTION>

This represents the caption for a table. CAPTION tags should appear inside the TABLE but not inside table rows or cells. The caption accepts an alignment attribute that defaults to ALIGN=top but can be explicitly set to ALIGN=bottom. Like table cells, any document body HTML can appear in a caption. Captions are always horizontally centered with respect to the table, and may have their lines broken to fit within the width of the table.

The Table Attributes

BORDER

This attribute appears in the TABLE tag. If present, borders are drawn around all table cells. If absent, there are no borders, but by default space is left for borders, so the same table with and without the BORDER attribute will have the same width.

ALIGN

If appearing inside a CAPTION, it controls whether the caption appears above or below the table, and can have the values top or bottom, defaulting to top.

If appearing inside a TR, TH, or TD, it controls whether text inside the table cell(s) is aligned to the left side of the cell, the right side of the cell, or centered within the cell. Values are left, center, and right.

VALIGN

Appearing inside a TR, TH, or TD, it controls whether text inside the table cell(s) is aligned to the top of the cell, the bottom of the cell, or vertically centered within the cell. It can also specify that all the cells in the row should be vertically aligned to the same baseline. Values are top, middle, bottom, and baseline.

NOWRAP

If this attribute appears in any table cell (TH or TD) it means the lines within this cell cannot be broken to fit the width of the cell. Be cautious in use of this attribute as it can result in excessively wide cells.

COLSPAN

This attribute can appear in any table cell (TH or TD) and it specifies how many columns of the table this cell should span. The default COLSPAN for any cell is 1.

ROWSPAN

This attribute can appear in any table cell (TH or TD) and it specifies how many rows of the table this cell should span. The default ROWSPAN for any cell is 1. A span that extends into rows that were never specified with a TR will be truncated.

A Little More Control

We found when creating tables that the creator inevitably wanted a little more control, especially when creating complex multiply nested tables. To this end we added a few more attributes that we are hoping to get into the continually evolving proposed HTML 3.0 spec.

BORDER=<value>

By allowing the BORDER attribute to take a value, document authors gain two things. First they gain the ability to emphasize some tables with respect to others — a table with a border of four containing a sub-table with a border of one looks much nicer than if they both share the same default border width. Second, by explicitly setting BORDER to zero they regain that space originally reserved for borders between cells, allowing particularly compact tables.

CELLSPACING=<value>

This is a new attribute for the TABLE tag. By default Netscape 1.1 uses a cell spacing of two. For those fussy about the look of their tables, this gives them a little more control. Like it sounds, cell spacing is the amount of space inserted between individual cells in a table.

CELLPADDING=<value>

This is a new attribute for the TABLE tag. By default Netscape 1.1 uses a cell padding of one. Cell padding is the amount of space between the border of the cell and the contents of the cell. Setting a cell padding of zero on a table with borders might look bad because the edges of the text could touch the cell borders.

```
<TABLE BORDER=0 CELLSPACING=0 CELLPADDING=0>
```

gives the most compact table possible.

WIDTH=<value_or_percent>

When this attribute appears with the TABLE tag it is used to describe the desired width of this table, either as an absolute width in pixels, or a percentage of document width. Ordinarily, complex heuristics are applied to tables and their cells to attempt to present a pleasing looking table. Setting the WIDTH attribute overrides those heuristics and instead effort is put into fitting the table into the desired width as specified. In some cases it might be impossible to fit all the table cells at the specified width, in which case Netscape 1.1 will try to get as close as possible.

When this attribute appears with either the TH or TD tag it is used to describe the desired width of the cell, either as an absolute width in pixels, or a percentage of table width. Ordinarily, complex heuristics are applied to table cells to attempt to present a pleasing looking table. Setting the WIDTH attribute overrides those heuristics for that cell and instead effort is put into fitting the cell into the desired width as specified. In some cases it might be impossible to fit all the table cells at the specified widths, in which case Netscape 1.1 will try to get as close as possible.

Stuff and Bother (The Details)

Blank cells that contain no displayable elements are not given borders. If you wish the appearance of an empty cell, but with borders, put either a blank line or a non-breaking space in the cell:

```
<td> </td>
```

or

```
<td><br></td>
```

The proposed HTML 3.0 spec allows you to abuse row and column spans to create tables whose cells must overlap. Don't do this; it looks awful.

You will eventually create a cell containing nothing but an image, and you will wonder why your image is not properly centered inside the cell. You probably wrote HTML like:

```
<td>
  <img src="url">
</td>
```

That extra white space inside your cell and around your image gets collapsed into single-space characters. And it is these spaces (whose baselines by default align with the bottom of the image) which are making your cell look lopsided. Try this instead:

```
<td><img src="url"></td>
```

The Table Sampler

This is intended to be a tutorial of tables by example. This covers most of the new tags in tables, though it doesn't necessarily show some of the really creative capabilities available in tables.

A Basic 3x2 Table

```
AB C
 DE F

<TABLE BORDER>
        <TR>
                <TD>A</TD> <TD>B</TD> <TD>C</TD>
        </TR>
        <TR>
                <TD>D</TD> <TD>E</TD> <TD>F</TD>
        </TR>
</TABLE>
```

Two Demonstrations of ROWSPAN

```
Item 1       Item 3
        Item 2
 Item 4       Item 5

<TABLE BORDER>
        <TR>
                <TD>Item 1</TD>
                <TD ROWSPAN=2>Item 2</TD>
                <TD>Item 3</TD>
        </TR>
        <TR>
                <TD>Item 4</TD> <TD>Item 5</TD>
        </TR>
</TABLE>

Item 2 Item 3 Item 4
 Item 1
        Item 5 Item 6 Item 7

<TABLE BORDER>
        <TR>
                <TD ROWSPAN=2>Item 1</TD>
                <TD>Item 2</TD> <TD>Item 3</TD> <TD>Item 4</TD>
        </TR>
        <TR>
                <TD>Item 5</TD> <TD>Item 6</TD> <TD>Item 7</TD>
        </TR>
</TABLE>
```

Demonstration of COLSPAN

```
Item 1Item 2
 Item 3Item 4 Item 5
```

```
<TABLE BORDER>
        <TR>
                <TD>Item 1</TD>
                <TD COLSPAN=2>Item 2</TD>
        </TR>
        <TR>
                <TD>Item 3</TD> <TD>Item 4</TD> <TD>Item 5</TD>
        </TR>
</TABLE>
```

Demonstration of Headers, <TH>

```
Head1Head2 Head3
 A    B    C
 D    E    F
```

```
<TABLE BORDER>
        <TR>
                <TH>Head1</TH> <TH>Head2</TH> <TH>Head3</TH>
        </TR>
        <TR>
                <TD>A</TD> <TD>B</TD> <TD>C</TD>
        </TR>
        <TR>
                <TD>D</TD> <TD>E</TD> <TD>F</TD>
        </TR>
</TABLE>
```

Demonstration of COLSPAN and Headers

```
Head1Head2
 A B  C  D
 E F  G  H
```

```
<TABLE BORDER>
        <TR>
                <TH COLSPAN=2>Head1</TH>
                <TH COLSPAN=2>Head2</TH>
        </TR>
        <TR>
```

```
                    <TD>A</TD>  <TD>B</TD>  <TD>C</TD>  <TD>D</TD>
        </TR>
        <TR>
                    <TD>E</TD>  <TD>F</TD>  <TD>G</TD>  <TD>H</TD>
        </TR>
</TABLE>
```

Demonstration of Multiple Headers, COLSPAN

```
Head1          Head2
 Head 3Head 4 Head 5 Head 6
 A      B      C      D
 E      F      G      H
```

```
<TABLE BORDER>
        <TR>
                    <TH COLSPAN=2>Head1</TH>
                    <TH COLSPAN=2>Head2</TH>
        </TR>
        <TR>
                    <TH>Head 3</TH>  <TH>Head 4</TH>
                    <TH>Head 5</TH>  <TH>Head 6</TH>
        </TR>
        <TR>
                    <TD>A</TD>  <TD>B</TD>  <TD>C</TD>  <TD>D</TD>
        </TR>
        <TR>
                    <TD>E</TD>  <TD>F</TD>  <TD>G</TD>  <TD>H</TD>
        </TR>
</TABLE>
```

Demonstration of Side Headers

```
Head1Item 1 Item 2 Item 3
 Head2Item 4 Item 5 Item 6
 Head3Item 7 Item 8 Item 9
```

```
<TABLE BORDER>
        <TR><TH>Head1</TH>
                <TD>Item 1</TD>  <TD>Item 2</TD>  <TD>Item 3</TD></TR>
        <TR><TH>Head2</TH>
                <TD>Item 4</TD>  <TD>Item 5</TD>  <TD>Item 6</TD></TR>
        <TR><TH>Head3</TH>
                <TD>Item 7</TD>  <TD>Item 8</TD>  <TD>Item 9</TD></TR>
</TABLE>
```

Demonstration of Side Headers, ROWSPAN

```
      Item 1 Item 2   Item 3 Item 4
 Head1
      Item 5 Item 6   Item 7 Item 8
 Head2Item 9 Item 10 Item 3 Item 11
```

```
<TABLE BORDER>
        <TR><TH ROWSPAN=2>Head1</TH>
          <TD>Item 1</TD> <TD>Item 2</TD> <TD>Item 3</TD> <TD>Item 4</TD>
        </TR>
        <TR><TD>Item 5</TD> <TD>Item 6</TD> <TD>Item 7</TD> <TD>Item 8</TD>
        </TR>
        <TR><TH>Head2</TH>
          <TD>Item 9</TD> <TD>Item 10</TD> <TD>Item 3</TD> <TD>Item 11</TD>
        </TR>
</TABLE>
```

Sample Table Using All of These

```
                Average
             Height Weight
      Males. 1.9    0.003
 Gender
      Females 1.7   0.002
```

```
<TABLE BORDER>
        <TR>     <TD><TH ROWSPAN=2></TH>
                 <TH COLSPAN=2>Average</TH></TD>
        </TR>
        <TR>     <TD><TH>Height</TH><TH>Weight</TH></TD>
        </TR>
        <TR>     <TH ROWSPAN=2>Gender</TH>
                 <TH>Males</TH><TD>1.9</TD><TD>0.003</TD>
        </TR>
        <TR>     <TH>Females</TH><TD>1.7</TD><TD>0.002</TD>
        </TR>
</TABLE>
```

Clever Uses of ROWSPAN/COLSPAN

```
 1 2
A
 3 4
C D
```

```
<TABLE BORDER>
        <TR>
                <TD ALIGN=center ROWSPAN=2 COLSPAN=2>A</TD>
                <TD>1</TD>
                <TD>2</TD>
        </TR>
        <TR>
                <TD>3</TD>
                <TD>4</TD>
        </TR>
        <TR>
                <TD ALIGN=center ROWSPAN=2 COLSPAN=2>C</TD>
                <TD ALIGN=center ROWSPAN=2 COLSPAN=2>D</TD>
        </TR>
        <TR>
        </TR>
</TABLE>
```

Adjusting Margins and Borders

A Table without Borders

```
Item 1      Item 3
      Item 2
Item 4      Item 5
```

```
<TABLE>
        <TR>     <TD>Item 1</TD> <TD ROWSPAN=2>Item 2</TD> <TD>Item 3</TD>
        </TR>
        <TR>     <TD>Item 4</TD> <TD>Item 5</TD>
        </TR>
</TABLE>
```

A Table with a Border of 10

```
Item 1 Item 2
Item 3 Item 4
```

```
<TABLE BORDER=10>
```

```
        <TR>      <TD>Item 1</TD> <TD> Item 2</TD>
        </TR>
        <TR>      <TD>Item 3</TD> <TD>Item 4</TD>
        </TR>
</TABLE>
```

CELLPADDING and CELLSPACING

```
    A   B   C

    D   E   F

<TABLE BORDER CELLPADDING=10 CELLSPACING=0>
        <TR>
                <TD>A</TD> <TD>B</TD> <TD>C</TD>
        </TR>
        <TR>
                <TD>D</TD> <TD>E</TD> <TD>F</TD>
        </TR>
</TABLE>

    A  B   C

    D  E   F

<TABLE BORDER CELLPADDING=0 CELLSPACING=10>
        <TR>
                <TD>A</TD> <TD>B</TD> <TD>C</TD>
        </TR>
        <TR>
                <TD>D</TD> <TD>E</TD> <TD>F</TD>
        </TR>
</TABLE>

    A     B      C

    D     E      F

<TABLE BORDER CELLPADDING=10 CELLSPACING=10>
        <TR>
                <TD>A</TD> <TD>B</TD> <TD>C</TD>
        </TR>
        <TR>
                <TD>D</TD> <TD>E</TD> <TD>F</TD>
        </TR>
</TABLE>
```

```
     A     B     C

     D     E     F
<TABLE BORDER=5 CELLPADDING=10 CELLSPACING=10>
        <TR>
                <TD>A</TD> <TD>B</TD> <TD>C</TD>
        </TR>
        <TR>
                <TD>D</TD> <TD>E</TD> <TD>F</TD>
        </TR>
</TABLE>
```

Alignment, Captions, and Subtables

Demonstration of Multiple Lines in a Table

```
     January       February       March

   This is cell 1   Cell 2        Another cell,
                                  cell 3

   Cell 4         and now this Cell 6
                  is cell 5

<TABLE BORDER>
        <TR>
                <TH>January</TH>
                <TH>February</TH>
                <TH>March</TH>
        </TR>
        <TR>
                <TD>This is cell 1</TD>
                <TD>Cell 2</TD>
                <TD>Another cell,<br> cell 3</TD>
        </TR>
        <TR>
                <TD>Cell 4</TD>
                <TD>and now this<br>is cell 5</TD>
                <TD>Cell 6</TD>
        </TR>
</TABLE>
```

ALIGN=left|right|center
Can be applied to individual cells or whole ROWs

```
        January            February            March

  all aligned center      Cell 2        Another cell,
                                           cell 3


       aligned rightaligned to center default,
                                         aligned left
```

```
<TABLE BORDER>
      <TR>
          <TH>January</TH>
          <TH>February</TH>
          <TH>March</TH>
      </TR>
      <TR ALIGN=center>
          <TD>all aligned center</TD>
          <TD>Cell 2</TD>
          <TD>Another cell,<br> cell 3</TD>
      </TR>
      <TR>
          <TD ALIGN=right>aligned right</TD>
          <TD ALIGN=center>aligned to center</TD>
          <TD>default,<br>aligned left</TD>
      </TR>
</TABLE>
```

VALIGN=top|bottom|middle
Can be applied to individual cells or whole ROWs:

```
      January              February             March
   all aligned to topand now this       Cell 3
                  is cell 2
   aligned to the top                  default alignment,
                  aligned to the bottom center
```

```
<TABLE BORDER>
      <TR>
              <TH>January</TH>
              <TH>February</TH>
              <TH>March</TH>
      </TR>
      <TR VALIGN=top>
          <TD>all aligned to top</TD>
```

```
            <TD>and now this<br>is cell 2</TD>
            <TD>Cell 3</TD>
        </TR>
        <TR>
            <TD VALIGN=top>aligned to the top</TD>
            <TD VALIGN=bottom>aligned to the bottom</TD>
            <TD>default alignment,<br>center</TD>
        </TR>
</TABLE>
```

CAPTION=top|bottom

A top CAPTION

```
    January     February       March

  This is cell 1Cell 2     Another cell,
                           cell 3
```

```
<TABLE BORDER>
<CAPTION ALIGN=top>A top CAPTION</CAPTION>
        <TR>
                <TH>January</TH>
                <TH>February</TH>
                <TH>March</TH>
        </TR>
        <TR>
                <TD>This is cell 1</TD>
                <TD>Cell 2</TD>
                <TD>Another cell,<br> cell 3</TD>
        </TR>
</TABLE>
```

```
    January     February       March

  This is cell 1Cell 2     Another cell,
                           cell 3
```

A bottom CAPTION

```
<TABLE BORDER>
<CAPTION ALIGN=bottom>A bottom CAPTION</CAPTION>
        <TR>
                <TH>January</TH>
                <TH>February</TH>
                <TH>March</TH>
```

```
            </TR>
            <TR>
                    <TD>This is cell 1</TD>
                    <TD>Cell 2</TD>
                    <TD>Another cell,<br> cell 3</TD>
            </TR>
    </TABLE>
```

Nested Tables: Table Abcd Is Inside Table 123456

```
      3
  12  A B
      C D


  45 6
```

```
<TABLE BORDER>
        <TR> <!-- ROW 1, TABLE 1 -->
                <TD>1</TD>
                <TD>2</TD>
                <TD>3
                <TABLE BORDER>
                        <TR> <!-- ROW 1, TABLE 2 -->
                                <TD>A</TD>
                                <TD>B</TD>
                        </TR>
                        <TR> <!-- ROW 2, TABLE 2 -->
                                <TD>C</TD>
                                <TD>D</TD>
                        </TR>
                </TABLE>
                </TD>
        </TR>
        <TR> <!-- ROW 2, TABLE 1 -->
                <TD>4</TD>
                <TD>5</TD>
                <TD>6</TD>
        </TR>
</TABLE>
```

Table Widths

```
BASIC 50% WIDTH

Width=50%          Width=50%
```

```
3                     4

<TABLE BORDER WIDTH="50%">
        <TR><TD>Width=50%</TD><TD>Width=50%</TD>
        </TR>
        <TR><TD>3</TD><TD>4</TD>
        </TR>
</TABLE>
```

Item Width Affects Cell Size

```
            2                 3                 4

<TABLE BORDER WIDTH="50%">
        <TR><TD>Item width affects cell size</TD><TD>2</TD>
        </TR>
        <TR><TD>3</TD><TD>4</TD>
        </TR>
</TABLE>

 WIDTH=100%                        This is item 2
 3                                 4

<TABLE BORDER WIDTH="100%">
        <TR><TD>WIDTH=100%</TD><TD>This is item 2</TD>
        </TR>
        <TR><TD>3</TD><TD>4</TD>
        </TR>
</TABLE>
```

Centering a Table on a Page

```
                    A         B         C
                    D         E         F

<CENTER>
<TABLE BORDER WIDTH="50%">
        <TR>
                <TD>A</TD> <TD>B</TD> <TD>C</TD>
        </TR>
        <TR>
                <TD>D</TD> <TD>E</TD> <TD>F</TD>
        </TR>
</TABLE>
</CENTER>
```

Table Width and Nested Tables

```
  Item 1                    Item 2


  Item A        Item B      Item 4
```

```
<TABLE BORDER WIDTH="50%">
        <TR><TD>Item 1</TD><TD>Item 2</TD>
        </TR>
        <TR><TD>
            <TABLE BORDER WIDTH=100%>
                <TR><TD>Item A</TD><TD>Item B</TD>
                </TR>
            </TABLE>
            </TD>
            <TD>Item 4</TD>
        </TR>
</TABLE>
HEIGHT=15%
HEIGHT=15%                  Item 2
  3                        4
```

```
<TABLE BORDER WIDTH="50%" HEIGHT="15%">
        <TR><TD>HEIGHT=15%</TD> <TD>Item 2</TD>
        </TR>
        <TR><TD>3</TD><TD>4</TD>
        </TR>
</TABLE>
```

[Image]

Controlling Document Backgrounds

The Background Attribute

Recent versions of the proposed HTML 3.0 spec have added a BACK-GROUND attribute to the BODY tag. The purpose of this attribute is to specify a URL pointing to an image that is to be used as a background for the document. In Netscape 1.1, this background image is used to tile the full background of the document-viewing area. Thus, specifying:

```
<BODY BACKGROUND="metal/brushed_aluminum.gif">Document here</BODY>
```

would cause whatever text, images, etc. appeared in that document to be placed on a background similar to the one at **http://www.netscape.com/ home/services_docs/html-extensions.html**. For more choices, take a look at a few examples at **http://home.netscape.com/assist/net_sites/bg/ backgrounds.html** for ideas on other backgrounds, or check out the helpful guide at **http://www.infi.net/wwwimages/colorindex.html** to various color swatches.

The BGCOLOR Attribute

This attribute to BODY is not currently in the proposed HTML 3.0 spec, but we're working on it. Basically, many people just want to change the color of the background without having to specify a separate image that requires another network access to load. This attribute allows just that. The format that Netscape 1.1 understands is:

```
<BODY BGCOLOR="#rrggbb">Document here</BODY>
```

Where "#rrggbb" is a hexadecimal red-green-blue triplet used to specify the background color.

How to Control the Document's Foreground

Clearly, once you have control of the background, you are going to need to also control the foreground to establish the proper contrasts. The following attributes are also recognized as part of the BODY tag by Netscape 1.1.

The TEXT Attribute

This attribute is used to control the color of all the normal text in the document. This basically consists of all text that is not specially colored to indicate a link. The format of TEXT is the same as that of BGCOLOR:

```
<BODY TEXT="#rrggbb">Document here</BODY>
```

The LINK, VLINK, and ALINK Attributes

These attributes let you control the coloring of link text. VLINK stands for visited link, and ALINK stands for active link. The default coloring of these is: LINK=blue, VLINK=purple, and ALINK=red. Again, the format for these attributes is the same as that for BGCOLOR and TEXT:

```
<BODY LINK="#rrggbb" VLINK="#rrggbb" ALINK="#rrggbb">Document
here</BODY>
```

Complete Example

```
<HTML>

<HEAD>
<TITLE>Color Control Example</TITLE>
</HEAD>

<BODY BGCOLOR="#000000" TEXT="#F0F0F0"
      LINK="#FFFF00" VLINK="#22AA22" ALINK="#0077FF">

This is an example document.  Text is light-gray on black, and
<a href="nowhere.html">anchors</a> are yellow at first,
flashing blue-green when activated, and pale green if already visited.
</P>
</BODY>

</HTML>
```

Stuff and Bother (The Details)

To state the obvious, since these color controls are all attributes of the BODY tag, you can only set the colors once for the entire document. You cannot change coloring partially through a document.

Since setting a background image requires the fetching of an image file from a second HTTP connection, it will slow down the perceived speed of your document load. None of your document can be displayed until the image is loaded and decoded. Needless to say, keep your background images small.

If you have the Auto Load Images option off, background images will not be loaded. If the background image is not loaded for any reason, and a BGCOLOR was not also specified, then any of the foreground controlling attributes (LINK, VLINK, and ALINK) will be ignored. The idea behind this is that if you didn't get your requested background image, setting your requested text colors on top of the default gray background may well make your document unreadable.

Appendix D

ENTITIES AND
ISO LATIN-1 CHARACTER ENTITIES

Here's some more HTML that you may need from time to time to do the unusual. We thought you'd like to have it all in a couple of pages. Have at it.

Entities

The following entity names are always prefixed by ampersand (&) and followed by a semicolon as shown.

<
  The less than sign, <

>
  The greater than sign, >

&

> The ampersand sign, &, itself.

"

> The double quote sign, "

** **

> A nonbreaking space

ISO Latin-1 Character Entities

This list is derived from "ISO 8879:1986//ENTITIES.

Æ

> capital AE diphthong (ligature), Æ

Á

> capital A, acute accent, Á

Â

> capital A, circumflex accent, Â

À

> capital A, grave accent, À

Å

> capital A, ring, Å

Ã

> capital A, tilde, Ã

Ä

> capital A, dieresis or umlaut mark, Ä

Ç
>   capital C, cedilla, Ç

Ð
>   capital Eth, Icelandic

É
>   capital E, acute accent, É

Ê
>   capital E, circumflex accent, Ê

È
>   capital E, grave accent, È

Ë
>   capital E, dieresis or umlaut mark, Ë

Í
>   capital I, acute accent, Í

Î
>   capital I, circumflex accent, Î

Ì
>   capital I, grave accent, Ì

Ï
>   capital I, dieresis or umlaut mark, Ï

Ñ
>   capital N, tilde, Ñ

Ó

    capital O, acute accent, Ó

Ô

    capital O, circumflex accent, Ô

Ò

    capital O, grave accent, Ò

Ø

    capital O, slash, Ø

Õ

    capital O, tilde, Õ

Ö

    capital O, dieresis or umlaut mark, Ö

Þ

    capital Thorn, Icelandic

Ú

    capital U, acute accent, Ú

Û

    capital U, circumflex accent, Û

Ù

    capital U, grave accent, Ù

Ü

    capital U, dieresis or umlaut mark, Ü

Ý
> capital Y, acute accent

á
> small a, acute accent, á

â
> small a, circumflex accent, â

æ
> small ae diphthong (ligature), æ

à
> small a, grave accent, à

å
> small a, ring, å

ã
> small a, tilde, ã

ä
> small a, dieresis or umlaut mark, ä

ç
> small c, cedilla, ç

é
> small e, acute accent, é

ê
> small e, circumflex accent, ê

è
>   small e, grave accent, è

ð
>   small eth, Icelandic

ë
>   small e, dieresis or umlaut mark, ë

í
>   small i, acute accent, í

î
>   small i, circumflex accent, î

ì
>   small i, grave accent, ì

ï
>   small i, dieresis or umlaut mark, ï

ñ
>   small n, tilde, ñ

ó
>   small o, acute accent, ó

ô
>   small o, circumflex accent, ô

ò
>   small o, grave accent, ò

ø
> small o, slash, ø

õ
> small o, tilde, õ

ö
> small o, dieresis or umlaut mark, ö

ß
> small sharp s, German (sz ligature), ß

þ
> small thorn, Icelandic

ú
> small u, acute accent, ú

û
> small u, circumflex accent, û

ù
> small u, grave accent, ù

ü
> small u, dieresis or umlaut mark, ü

ý
> small y, acute accent

ÿ
> small y, dieresis or umlaut mark, ÿ

Appendix E

THE WEBMASTER TOOLKIT

HTML Editors for Windows 3.x, 95, NT

Ant HTML
>	MS Word 6.0 unchecked WYSIWYG template
>	Author: Jill Swift (jswift@freenet.fsu.edu)
>	Cost: Free (noncommercial use)
>
>	**ftp://ftp.uoknor.edu/mirrors/networking/info-service/www/ncsa/html/Windows**

CU HTML
>	MS Word unchecked WYSIWYG template
>	Cost: Free (noncommercial use)
>	Authors: Kenneth Wong and Anton Lam (anton-lam@cuhk.hk)
>
>	**http://www.cuhk.hk/csc/cu_html/cu_html.htm**

The HotDog Web Editor

Raw text stand-alone unchecked editor
Cost: $29 US
Author: Sausage Software (sales@sausage.com)

http://www.sausage.com

Supports both HTML 3 and Netscape. Customizable, very attractive. Win95-style interface even on "normal" Windows. Tons of time-saving features. Please see our Web site to find out why everyone's raving about HotDog!

HoTMetaL

WYSIWYG stand-alone rule-based editor
Cost: Free (commercial version available)
Author: SoftQuad (info@sq.com)

http://www.sq.com/

This is a very basic HTML editor, with few redeeming qualities when compared to some other available packages. Creating new documents can be confusing, especially if one has used any other editor. The standard method of selecting text and defining it does not work here: the tag must be selected first, then text inserted. The tags are graphical and more noticeable, and the text appears as it would when viewed with a browser. Unfortunately, there are no buttons for quick formatting: all tags are in one master list, which must be scrolled through and selected. The ability to view the document's link and structure helps in visualization, yet no editing in these views is allowed. Overall, this editor is difficult to use efficiently. It may be of use to the completely uninitiated HTML writer, but its usefulness does not extend beyond that.

HTMLed Pro Version 1.0*

Stand-alone unchecked editor
Cost: $39 US (shareware)
Author: Internet Software Technologies

http://www.ist.c a

This package has many user-friendly features which make the creation of HTML documents quick and easy for an experienced HTML programmer, such as the option to start new documents with a modifiable and storable template of the standard HEAD, HTML, and BODY tags. Custom toolbars are useful for working with HTML 3.0 (which is fully supported in this version) and creating other custom tags. Dialog boxes make form and table creation a breeze. Adding links is simplified by the ability to browse the local disk for links. Overall, the experienced HTML programmer will find this package a good, basic editor.

HTML Assistant V1.4*

Stand-alone unchecked editor
Cost: Free (Pro version $99 US)
Author: H Harawitz (sales@brooknorth.bedford.ns.ca)

http://fox.nstn.ca/~harawitz/index.html

Defining text is made simple by a dialog box, which the user scrolls through and selects for insertion into a page. All the normal URLs are supported in a simple dialog. Browsing local files is supported, which really is a must. Creating named anchors is made easy with a simplified dialog, and browsing local files is supported. HTML 3.0 is not supported but they can easily be inserted into a custom tag list. Unfortunately, the beginning HTML programmer will find many

---

* Asterisks denote items that are included on the CD-ROM that accompanies this book.

features confusing, because the package provides only limited information on how tags should be used. Inconsistency in the presentation of tags is a problem. Where one tag will have the name (i.e., <pre>) with an accompanying description, others will just be named by their effect. This package is an excellent HTML editor, but more flexible customization is needed (and available in the Pro version).

HTML Author

MS Word 6.0 unchecked WYSIWYG template
Some validity checking
Cost: Freeware
Author: Grahame Cooper (G.S.Cooper@iti.salford.ac.uk)

http://www.salford.ac.uk/docs/depts/iti/staff/gsc/htmlauth/ summary.html

Specialized toolbars. Paragraph and character styles defined using Word styles. Dialogue box maintenance of anchors using pick lists. Jump (forward and backward) to referenced documents, anchors and pictures for editing. Automatically generated hypertext table of contents and page owner details.

HTML Handler

Stand-alone unchecked editor
Cost: Freeware
Author: Jon Reinberg (reinb001@maroon.tc.umn.edu)

http://www.umn.edu/nlhome/m447/reinb001/hthand.html

HTML HyperEdit 0.4a

Stand alone unchecked editor
Cost: Freeware
Author: Steve Hancock (s.hancock@icarus.curtin.edu.au)

http://www.curtin.edu.au/curtin/dept/cc/packages/htmledit/home.html

This is a bare bones editor in some respects, yet very specialized in others. Provided tags are minimal, yet the user can add tags to a scroll-down menu. There is no HTML 3.0 support, but the customization makes up for this somewhat. The link dialog box is very complex, yet understandable. It makes creation of different links easy and quick. A very interesting feature is the "signature" button, where the user can define a "sig" or a nav bar and insert it with one click into any document. Only one signature at a time can be defined, however. This editor does not support testing of new documents. The user can toggle between "beginner" and "advanced" features. Overall, this is a basic, sometimes cryptic, yet usable editor.

HTML Writer 0.9 Beta 4a

Stand-alone unchecked editor
Cost: Donationware
Author: Kris Nosack (html-writer@byu.edu)

http://lal.cs.byu.edu/people/nosack

This is a clean, impressive HTML editor. The template feature greatly facilitates the creation of new documents. Insertion of images and links are also made easier by clear and specific dialog boxes. The user interface is attractive and logical, yet no customization is allowed. Because the editor does not support HTML 3.0, these tags must be inserted manually.

Internet Assistant

MS Word 6.0 template
Cost: Freeware
Author: Microsoft Corporation

http://www.microsoft.com/pages/deskapps/word/ia/default.htm

Live Markup 0.95B3

MS-Windows editor
Stand-alone program
Cost: $29 US (shareware)

http://www.mediatec.com/mediatech/

WebEdit 1.0

Stand-alone unchecked editor
Cost: $99.95 US (shareware)
Author: Kenn Nesbitt (kennn@netcom.com)

http://www.thegroup.net/webedit.htm

Thankfully, this editor package provides support for most of HTML 3.0 and Netscape Extensions. The user interface is extremely friendly and intuitive, and useful for both beginners and seasoned HTML programmers. The dialogs for links and images are excellent, including the capacity for a complete list of URL types, image options, and file browsing. The lack of extensive user customization is offset by the HTML 3.0 support. However, all markup requires two clicks (select the type, then the actual tag) instead of one in a tool bar. Overall, this is an excellent editor, which I found the easiest and most efficient to use.

WebWizard

Stand-alone unchecked raw editor
Cost: Freeware
Author: David Geller / ARTA Software Group (davidg@halcyon.com)

http://www.halcyon.com/webwizard/

Graphics Tools for Windows 3.X, 95, NT

To create interlaced images:

Graphics Workshop for Windows

http://uunorth.north.net:8000/alchemy/html/gww.html

WinGIF v1.4

Cost: $15 US (shareware)
Author: Kyle Powell (76704.12@compuserve.com)

ftp://ftp.best.com/pub/craig/windows_apps/wingif14.zip

Windows image viewer/enhancer to create both interlaced and transparent images.

GIF Construction Set for Windows

http://uunorth.north.net:8000/alchemy/html/gifcon.html

LView Pro 1.B*

Cost: $30 US (shareware)
Author: John Fulmer (jfulmer@databank.com)

ftp://oak.oakland.edu/SimTel/win3/graphics/lviewp1b.zip

Full-featured graphics maniuplator.

Paint Shop Pro

Cost: Shareware

ftp://oak.oakland.edu/SimTel/win3/graphics/psp30.zip

Full-featured graphics manipulator.

VuePrint

Cost: $40 US
Author: Hamrick Software (EdHamrick@aol.com)

http://www.primenet.com/~hamrick

Full-featured graphic, sound, movie player/viewer and graphic manipulator.

SnapShot/32*

Cost: $20 US (shareware)
Author: Greg Kochaniak (greg@kagi.com)

http://198.207.242.3/gregko/snap32.htm

A screen-capture utility that offers T/I GIF output to create image-maps.

MapEdit 1.4

Cost: $25 US (shareware)
Author: Thomas Boutell (boutell@netcom.com)

ftp://ftp.best.com/pub/schaft/HTML_Stuff/webedt11.zip

Map THIS!*

Cost: Freeware
Author: Todd C. Wilson (tc@galadriel.ecaetc.ohio-state.edu)

http://galadriel.ecaetc.ohio-state.edu/tc/mt/

An imagemap creator/editor.

Sound and Movies

GOLDWAVE*
>   Cost: Shareware
>   Author: Chris Craig (chris3@garfield.cs.mun.ca)

>   ftp://ftp.cdrom.com/.22/cica/sounds/gldwav21.zip

>   Sound editor, player and recorder.

MPEGPLAY v1.61*
>   Cost: $25 US (shareware)
>   Author: Michael Simmons (michael@ecel.uwa.edu.au)

>   http://www.geom.umn.edu/docs/mpeg_play/mpeg_play.html

WHAM (Waveform Hold and Modify) 1.31*
>   Cost: $20–30 US (shareware)
>   Author: Andrew Bulhak (acb@yoyo.cc.monash.edu.au)

>   ftp://ftp.cdrom.com/.22/cica/sounds/wham133.zip

>   Can read and write Windows 3.1 WAVE files, raw eight-bit digitized
>   sound files and files of several other formats (of which more may be
>   added) and can perform various operations on this sound.

Windows Play Any File, version 1.1
>   Cost: Freeware
>   Author: Bill Neisius (bill@solaria.hac.com).

>   ftp://ftp.cdrom.com/.22/cica/sounds/wplny11.zip

>   Will detect and play any sound file through a Windows 3.1 audio
>   device.

Utilities

(These are easy enough to download.)

PK Unzip (for .zip files)

http://www.primenet.com/~hamrick/files/pkunzip.exe

Video for Windows 1.1e

http://www.primenet.com/~hamrick/files/vfw11e.exe

VMPEG Viewer for MPEG Files

http://www.primenet.com/~hamrick/files/vmpeg16.zip

Win32s Extension for Windows

http://www.primenet.com/~hamrick/files/win32s12.exe

Win32s Installation Problem Solving

http://www.primenet.com/~hamrick/files/win32spr.txt

WS_FTP (FTP-32 Client for Windows)

ftp://winftp.cica.indiana.edu/pub/pc/win3/winsock/WS_ftp.zip

ftp://winftp.cica.indiana.edu/pub/pc/win3/winsock/WS_ftp32.zip

Appendix F

ANNOUNCING YOUR WWW SITE AND THEN SOME

This is the last appendix. It may also be the most useful. This is where you'll find out how to announce your new WWW site and where you'll find the location of almost every Windows-related resource on the Net.

Extra special thanks (yet again!) to Carl de Cordova and Jon Wieder-span for helping us pull this all together. Thanks to them, this appendix contains just about every Webmaster Windows-related newsgroup, mailing list, WWW site, FTP site, FAQ, and journal in the universe. Or at least most of them.

Announcing Your Site

The best place to go to announce your site is Jon Wiederspan's WWW server at:

> http://www.uwtc.washington.edu/Computing/WWW/
> AnnouncingYourSite.html

He's got a comprehensive list of pointers including the one to the Submit It! WWW Server at:

> http://www.cen.uiuc.edu/~banister/submit-it/

If you go to the Submit It! WWW server and register your site there, you'll cover all the bases in one shot.

Useful WWW-related Newsgroups, Mailing Lists, and WWW Sites for Windows WebMasters

You can find the list of all the useful WWW newsgroups and mailing lists at:

> http://www.uwtc.washington.edu/Computing/WWW/
> WebListsAndGroups.html.

Señor Wiederspan has done a nice job of pulling this all together.

Useful WWW Newsgroups

- comp.infosystems.www.users provides a forum for discussion of WWW client software (such as Mosaic, Cello and Lynx). New use questions, client setup questions, client bug reports, resource discovery questions on how to locate information on WWW that can't be found by the FAQ, and comparisons between various client packages are among the acceptable topics for this group.

- comp.infosystems.www.providers provides a forum for the discussion of WWW server software and the use of server software to provide information to users. General server design, setup questions, server bug reports, security issues, HTML page design, and other concerns of information providers are among the likely topics for this group.

- comp.infosystems.www.misc provides a general forum for discussing WWW issues not covered by the other comp.infosystems. www groups.

- comp.infosystems.announce is for announcement of new information services (e.g., new WWW sites) and new software products (new server software, new clients, new document convertors, etc.).
- alt.hypertext has less traffic than the comp.infosystems.www groups but is also less "professional."
- comp.infosystems.gopher provides a forum for discussing Gopher, but sometimes covers WWW issues.
- comp.infosystems.wais covers WAIS topics, including integration of WAIS with WWW.
- comp.text.sgml covers SGML, including HTML.

Useful WWW Mailing Lists

www-announce

General discussion about the World Wide Web.

Server: listserv@info.cern.ch

Send e-mail with one line in the body containing:

```
subscribe www-announce your_name
```

www-html

Technical discussions of the HyperText Markup Language (HTML) and HTMLPlus designs.

Server: listserv@info.cern.ch

Send e-mail with one line in the body containing:

```
subscribe www-html your_name
```

www-talk

Technical discussion for those developing WWW software or with that deep an interest.

Server: listserv@info.cern.ch

Send e-mail with one line in the body containing:

```
subscribe www-talk your_name
```

www-rdb

Discussion of gatewaying relational databases into WWW.

Server: listserv@info.cern.ch

Send e-mail with one line in the body containing:

```
subscribe www-rdb your_name
```

www-proxy

Technical discussion about WWW proxies, caching, and future directions.

Server: listserv@info.cern.ch

Send e-mail with one line in the body containing:

```
subscribe www-proxy your_name
```

web-support

A Mailbase list that can be used for discussions about WWW issues.

Server: mailbase@mailbase.ac.uk

Send e-mail with one line in the body stating:

```
join web-support your_name
```

uctlig-infs

A Mailbase list that can be used for discussions about information systems, including WWW.

Server: mailbase@mailbase.ac.uk

Send e-mail with one line in the body stating:

```
join uctlig-infs your_name
```

unite

A Mailbase list that can be used for discussions about a User Network Interface To Everything. UNITE is available as an archive at mailbase@mailbase.ac.uk. Send e-mail with one line in the body containing:

```
join unite your_name
```

Final Words

As they say in LooneyTunes, "That's All Folks." We hope you've had as good a time with it as we have.

Bob LeVitus & Jeff Evans

INDEX

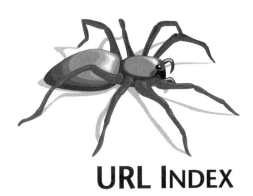

URL Index

QUARTERDECK WEBSERVER TRIALWARE

Release 1.0

This document contains important information that may not be available in the Quarterdeck WebServer manual or on-line Help.

How This Trialware Works

Quarterdeck WebServer trialware is a full-featured product that expires 30 days from the time you initially install it. You may purchase Quarterdeck WebServer at any time during those 30 days by closing down the Web server and following the on-screen instructions (modem required) or by contacting Quarterdeck directly at (800) 354-3222. You will be able to purchase Quarterdeck WebServer for a reduced price of $119.95, plus shipping and handling charges, and will receive a full product by mail.

Overview

Thank you for trying Quarterdeck's WebServer for Windows! We at Quarterdeck Corporation are proud to offer version 1.0 of the Quarterdeck WebServer. This is just one of Quarterdeck's Internet line of products that makes it easy to publish and find information on the Internet, as well as send and receive electronic mail. Quarterdeck is well known for making computing easier by creating products for the beginner as well as the expert user. The Quarterdeck WebServer is no exception to this.

Using the Quarterdeck WebServer, you can set up your own personal Internet Web site. The Quarterdeck WebServer is also ideal for intracompany use, such as serving up human resource policies. When using the WebServer as an intracompany Web server, an Internet connection is not required.

Once the Quarterdeck WebServer is installed, you can use WebAuthor, Quarterdeck's HTML authoring tool, to create and maintain your Web site's HTML documents. If you are shopping for a Web browser product, please try Quarterdeck's QMosaic.

Quarterdeck WebServer features include:

- A graphical user interface (WebServer Setup Utility) that allows you to easily customize your Web server for administration/logging, document management, user access, script management, and network configuration
- Thorough on-line help, written documentation, and sample Web pages
- Support for 16 simultaneous connections
- Efficient, cooperative multi-threading design that eliminates the need for a dedicated server machine
- Support for Image maps and fill-out forms
- Log files that track all WebServer activity
- WinSock 1.1 compliance
- Support for asynchronous processing

One way in which you can help us make this the best product of its kind is to let us know what you think! If you have a feature that you think we should add, or even a minor suggestion, please do not hesitate to let us know. We always listen to our customers! Your feedback allows us to create even better products.

You can contact Quarterdeck via the following eMail addresses:

Technical Questions and Comment:	SUPPORT@QDECK.COM
Product Information	INFO@QDECK.COM
General WebServer and World Wide Web Questions	WEBMASTER@QDECK.COM

Installation and Setup Notes

The Quarterdeck WebServer comes with an automated installation program that completes all necessary WebServer configuration for you, as part of the installation. When the WebServer installation has completed, simply reboot your machine, restart windows and you are ready to run the WebServer.

When installing the WebServer on a LAN-based network (with or without Internet connectivity), the WebServer requires a TCP/IP stack with a 1.1 compliant WinSock. Internet connectivity is not required if you plan to use the WebServer as an intracompany Web server. If you do not already have a TCP/IP stack, you can chose to install the LAN Work Place TCP/IP stack that comes with the Quarterdeck WebServer. The installation of the TCP/IP stack has been integrated into the WebServer installation as an optional component.

If you plan on making your WebServer available on the Internet via a dial-up connection (phone line), you must have a SLIP/PPP-based Internet account. When you establish a SLIP/PPP account, your Internet service provider will supply you with the actual SLIP/PPP software. This SLIP/PPP software must be used in place of the TCP/IP software that is provided with the WebServer. The TCP/IP software supplied with the WebServer is not compatible with a dial-up connection.

To make your Web site publicly available on the Internet, you must have an Internet connection. If you do not already have an Internet connection, you can establish one through your local Internet service provider (ISP). There are a number of options available when it comes to choosing the type of Internet connection you want. Some of the more common ways to connect to the Internet include modem connection, ISDN connection, fractional T1 connection and full T1 connection. To obtain more information on these options, contact your local Internet service provider.

Windows NT 3.5 and Windows 95 Support

The Quarterdeck WebServer for Windows 3.x will run as a 16-bit application under Windows NT 3.5 and the current Windows 95 beta.

Stay tuned to Quarterdeck for information on Quarterdeck's new 32 bit WebServer for Windows NT and Windows 95 which will be available later this year.

Tips for Internet Use

If you plan on connecting your WebServer to the Internet, you can tune its performance by doing the following:

- Use the WebServer Setup utility to disable the "Fancy Listings" feature found on the Directory Listings screen. Disabling this option prevents icons from being used in server-generated directory listings. When icons are used in directory listings, each icon requires a separate request from the Web browser. Turning off this option reduces the number of server requests required to create a directory listing.
- Use the "-i" command line parameter when starting the Web-Server. This will disable the "host name lookup" feature. By default, when the WebServer receives a request, it does a "host name lookup" to retrieve the name associated with the address of the host making the request. The host name, rather than the IP address, is used in the WebServer log files. WebServer performance can be significantly improved by disabling this feature. When this feature is disabled, full IP addresses, rather than host names, must be specified when defining security access permissions. In addition, IP addresses will be used in the WebServer log files.

Setting the Time Zone Environment Variable

You can customize the Time Zone environment variable to accommo-date Daylight Savings Time by changing the Time Zone value set by the WebServer installation process to the following format:

```
TZ=tnz[+ | -]hh[:mm[:ss] ][dzn]
```

where *tnz* is a three-letter time-zone name such as PST, followed by an optionally signed number, + – hh, that gives the difference in hours between Universal Coordinated Time (UCT) and local time.

To specify the exact local time, the hours can be followed by min-utes (mm), seconds (ss), and a three-letter daylight-saving-time zone (dzn) such as PDT.

Example: PST8PDT would represent Pacific Standard Time, 8 hours offset from UCT, Pacific Daylight Savings Time.

Troubleshooting Tips

Following are anwers to frequently asked questions regarding the Quar-terdeck WebServer.

The WebServer will not start. How can I determine what is wrong?
During initialization processing the WebServer creates a log, HTTPD.LOG, in its installation root directory. This log will contain an error message explaining why the WebServer was not able to successfully start. The most common WebServer startup problem is a missing Time Zone environment variable (TZ).

The WebServer will not start and the log file contains a WSA... error message (WinSock error message).
You do not have enough conventional memory available to run the WebServer.

Nothing happens when I press the Keyword button on the Setup utility main window.

Once the Keyword dialog has been activated, it can become hidden behind other windows, giving the impression that it has been closed. However, when you try to open it again, it appears to not start. This is because it is already open but hidden behind another window.

The WebServer demonstration contained in the sample Web pages does not work.

Make sure that you are not viewing the sample Web pages in your browser's local file mode. When viewing the sample WebServer HTML documents use the scheme "http:" to access to sample WebServer HTML documents.

For example, from your Web browser, open the following URL:

```
http://yourserver/index.htm
```

where *yourserver* is the name of the server machine that the WebServer is running on.

Name _____

Company _____

Address _____

City _____ State _____ ZIP Code _____

Phone _____ Fax _____

PPP Account Number: _____

One Free Month of

UUNET's AlterDial

Service

AlterDial and UUNET are registered
trademarks of UUNET Technologies, Inc.

This *free* month of UUNET's AlterDial® service is a limited-time introductory offer, which allows <u>WebMaster</u> purchasers to receive AlterDial service free for one month, including up to fifteen (15) hours of connect time. Connect time in excess of the fifteen free hours will be billed at UUNET's current rates. UUNET's standard $25 start-up fee will still apply.

To establish service, you must either sign and return an AlterDial subscription form or autoregister for the service using our special software. For more information, or to receive the software, please call UUNET Technologies, Inc., at **+1 800 265 0499**. You must return this original coupon after receipt of your first bill to obtain the credit. Photocopies and facsimiles of this coupon are not acceptable. Your credit card may be billed; however, we will issue you a credit as soon as we receive this coupon.

Billing is automatic. You must cancel the service before the start of any additional months if you do not wish to continue service. Use of this coupon does not waive any of the standard terms and conditions found on the reverse side of the AlterDial subscription form.

This offer is restricted to **new** UUNET customers only. Only one coupon per customer will be accepted. This offer may be revised or rescinded at any time, and is valid only in the continental United States. Monthly service fees and hourly connection charges are subject to change per the standard AlterDial Terms and Conditions. This coupon expires July 31, 1996.

Name _____

Company _____

Address _____

City _____ State _____ ZIP Code _____

Phone _____ Fax _____

$100 off UUNET's

Web Server Hosting

Start-up Fee

This coupon entitles <u>WebMaster</u> purchasers to a $100 discount off the normal start-up fee for UUNET's Web server hosting services.

UUNET's Web server hosting services provide you with an easy and affordable way to establish and maintain your company's presence on the World Wide Web. Both our Standard and Premium services offer a low price for the first month that we host your server, and include usage reports showing activity for your server "pages." At your request, UUNET can also develop your server content, providing a fully-integrated service.

To establish service, you must complete a Web Hosting Subscription Form and a Web Hosting Configuration Form. When you receive your first invoice, you must attach this original coupon and return it to us to receive the $100 credit. Photocopies and facsimiles of this coupon are not acceptable. For more information or to sign up, please call UUNET Technologies at **+1 800 258 4039**.

This offer is restricted to **new** UUNET customers only. Only one coupon per customer will be accepted. This offer may be revised or rescinded at any time, and is valid only in the continental United States. This coupon expires July 31, 1996.

UUNET is a registered trademark of UUNET Technologies, Inc.

UUNET's **AlterDial** service connects your desktop or laptop computer directly to the Internet, the world's greatest source of communications and information. Through your link to UUNET's international network you can travel the World Wide Web, send e-mail, log in to remote computers, transfer files, participate in newsgroup discussions, and retrieve valuable information from countless global databases.

AlterDial supplies Internet access to your office or home, providing a total networking solution to small businesses, telecommuters, and employees in the field. You need only a modem, a standard analog phone line, and software implementing the PPP protocol, all of which are available through UUNET. And depending on your usage requirements, you can choose billing by connect time or at a fixed monthly rate.

AlterDial represents the state of the art in dial-up Internet connectivity. AlterDial permits multiple user mailboxes and registration of your own unique domain name. Traveling users can seamlessly connect to any of UUNET's hubs around the country, or to a convenient 800 number. UUNET's industry-leading *experience, network connectivity, and support* add business-class reliability that you will find in no other Internet service provider.

For more information, please call UUNET Technologies at **+1 800 265 0499** and mention this coupon.

UUNET Technologies, Inc.
3060 Williams Drive, Fairfax, Virginia 22031-4648 USA (Attn: Accounting)
info@uu.net
http://www.uu.net

UUNET brings the **World Wide Web** to your business with a no-hassle turnkey solution, consisting of:

- **Facilities management**
  Your Web pages can be stored on a dedicated server on our site. You don't need to worry about hardware, software, or anything else—we take care of everything! The server is monitored and maintained 24 hours a day, 365 days a year, by our Network Operations Center, protected by an Uninterruptible Power Supply with backup generator. This means you never need to worry about potential customers not being able to get your information. And since we maintain the machine at our facilities, there are no security concerns for you.
- **High-speed server response, even at peak times**
  Since your Web server is directly connected to our backbone, you won't experience the poor performance associated with limited bandwidth or network capacity. You may choose from connection speeds of either T-1 (1.544 Mbps) or 10 Mbps, ensuring the fastest possible response times for those accessing your pages.
- **Usage feedback**
  We will provide regular usage statistics reports for you, giving you valuable feedback on how many users are accessing your Web pages, and what they're looking at the most.
- **Content services**
  All you need to provide is the information that you would like to make available to your audience. Working with our development partners, we will convert existing text, arrange the structure of the information to suit the WWW medium, and format the material and graphics to reflect your corporate identity. We'll create compelling graphics to get you noticed! In addition, we will keep your information up to date.

The World Wide Web is the fastest-growing way to reach Internet users—don't be left behind!

For more information, please call UUNET Technologies at **+1 800 258 4039** and mention this coupon.

UUNET Technologies, Inc.
3060 Williams Drive, Fairfax, Virginia 22031-4648 USA (Attn: Accounting)
info@uu.net
http://www.uu.net

About the CD-ROM

The CD-ROM packaged with this book contains the following software for setting up your Web site.

HTML Editors

HTMLed Pro Version 1.0	A stand-alone unchecked editor
HTML Assistant V1.4	A stand-alone unchecked editor

Graphics Tools

LView Pro 1.B	A full-featured graphics manipulator
SnapShot/32	A screen-capture utility that offers GIF output to create imagemaps
Map THIS!	An imagemap creator/editor

Sound and Movie Tools

GOLDWAVE	Sound editor, player, and recorder
MPEGPLAY v1.61	Sound player
WHAM 1.31	Sound editor, player, and recorder

Web server

Quarterdeck WebServer 1.0	Trialware server

System Requirements

Windows PC running Windows 3.1 or later
CD-ROM drive